# PRAISE FOR *VISIT FROM HEAVEN*

*Visit from Heaven* is Alicia Young's riveting account of her personal spiritual experiences related to the prospect of life after death. Her book is a treasure trove of interesting information about near-death experiences, shared-death experiences, and reincarnation. My personal favorite is her discussion of the planning that occurs prior to birth into this life, a topic that also fascinated Plato, who inspired my inquiry into the afterlife. I am certain that you will enjoy reading Ms. Young's book as much as I did.

—Dr. Raymond Moody, author of the international best seller *Life After Life,* lifeafterlife.com

With tenderness, insight, and grace, Alicia Young expands our knowledge of our nonphysical Home and the pre-birth planning we do there. For anyone seeking to understand why we are here on earth, this book is highly recommended.

—Rob Schwartz, Between Lives Soul Regression therapist and author of *Your Soul's Plan* and *Your Soul's Gift,* yoursoulsplan.com

We both read Alicia's manuscript and enjoyed it greatly. She has done an excellent job. It's lovely, well written, and never boring!

*Visit from Heaven* is an insightful account of the wonderful way the spirit world can impact those of us on earth. Alicia has drawn thoughtful and inspiring conclusions from her personal experience, and is brave enough to put them out there in an attempt to bring understanding and healing to her readers.

—Michelle and Ezio De Angelis, mediums and Australian Psychics of the Year 2018, 2015, 2012; authors of *Postcards from the Other Side: True Stories of the Afterlife,* eziodeangelis.com.au (Sydney)

*Visit from Heaven* is an intriguing adventure offered by Alicia Young reflecting her personal experiences of this world and the next. As a hospice nurse, I have heard of otherworldly experiences from the families of dying children and adults in my care.

I approach Alicia's book with the same openness I came to understand through listening to the words of many grieving parents and siblings whose loved ones had died. God places us in experiences like Alicia's to teach us one more thing He wants us to know. His love never ends.

—TRUDY HARRIS, RN, FORMER SENIOR HOSPICE NURSE
AND AUTHOR OF *GLIMPSES OF HEAVEN: TRUE STORIES
OF HOPE AND PEACE AT THE END OF LIFE'S JOURNEY*

Alicia Young has done it again! With simple elegance and thought-provoking prose, *Visit from Heaven* is a compelling experience from the Other Side that is instructive in how to live our lives on earth.

—JODY LONG, NEAR DEATH EXPERIENCE
RESEARCH FOUNDATION, NDERF.ORG

I strongly recommend Alicia Young's book. It is clear to me from my investigations into language and consciousness that there are mysteries that exist that we do not understand fully, and among them are very real communications between the living and the dead—and even the unborn.

Alicia Young writes with tenderness and gentle conviction, in a way that opens the portal to those who do and those who don't believe that such things are possible. Read her book if you are at all curious about what might exist beyond the Veil and how readily accessible it may be after all. *Visit from Heaven* is a beautiful and inspiring tale that will stir in every reader a kind of remembrance of what it means to be a "soul."

—LISA SMARTT, FOUNDER OF THE FINAL WORDS PROJECT
AND AUTHOR OF *WORDS AT THE THRESHOLD: WHAT WE SAY AS
WE'RE NEARING DEATH*, FINALWORDSPROJECT.ORG

# VISIT FROM HEAVEN

# TITLES BY ALICIA YOUNG

(Yes, the topics are eclectic—but so is life!)

*Visit from Heaven:*
*A Soul's Message of Love, Loss & Family*
(2019)

*The Mother Teresa Effect:*
*What I Learned Volunteering for a Saint*
(2016)

*Two Eggs, Two Kids:*
*An Egg Donor's Account of Friendship, Infertility & Secrets*
(2015)

*The Savvy Bride's Guide:*
*Simple Ways to a Stylish & Graceful Wedding*
(2015, 2014)

*The Savvy Bride's Guide: Your Wedding Checklist*
(2015, 2014)

*The Savvy Girl's Guide to Grace:*
*Small Touches with Big Impact—at Home, Work & in Love*
(2013)

# VISIT FROM HEAVEN

## A SOUL'S MESSAGE OF LOVE, LOSS & FAMILY

ALICIA YOUNG

PARASOL PRESS
Asheville, NC, and Perth, WA

Publisher's Cataloging-in-Publication Data
Young, Alicia, author.
Visit from heaven : a soul's message of love, loss, and family / Alicia Young.
p. cm.
Includes bibliographical references and index.
LCCN 2018912139
ISBN 978-0-9965388-5-5 (pbk.)
ISBN 978-0-9965388-6-2 (ebook)
ISBN 978-0-6481639-2-3 (pbk., Aust.)
ISBN 978-0-6481639-3-0 (ebook, Aust.)
1. Spirituality. 2. Astral projection. 3. Reincarnation.
4. Self-help. 5. Miscarriage. 6. Bereavement. I. Title.
BF1261.2 .Y67 2018
DDC 133.9—dc23

PARASOL PRESS
Australia: PO Box 6254, Swanbourne, WA 6010
United States: Asheville, NC 28805
Email: info@parasolpress.net

aliciayoung.net

Book design by Monroe Street Studios
Cover art by happyvector071 via CanStockPhoto.com
Author photo by Elizabeth Shrier © 2016 Alicia Young
Parasol Press logo by Marcelo Gómez Oróstica

Printed in the United States of America and Australia
First printing 2019
10 9 8 7 6 5 4 3 2 1

*To Jane and Joe,
for their uncommon grace
in allowing me to
share this experience.*

A college student was on the radio, recounting his near-death experience. He had almost lost his life when he crashed his motorcycle while speeding, something his father lectured him on daily. As he left his body and surveyed the wreckage, he thought, "Dad's going to kill me!"

He added that he felt no pain, as his soul had left his physical body moments before the crash. This strikes me as a simple but potent insight. I hope it might ease the grief of those who have lost loved ones in traumatic circumstances.

As I listened, I could not have known I would one day experience a glimpse of the afterlife myself, through an out-of-body experience. I would come to consider this interview from a different angle: that the young man had planned his motorcycle accident as a potential departure point from this life.

In the following pages, I explain how I came to believe that we choose certain events in our lives, and the key people in them.

Surprisingly, it would be a little boy who would turn my thinking upside down.

# CONTENTS

# PREFACE

At its core, *Visit from Heaven* is about an encounter in which the soul of a little boy, Bobby, visited me from the afterlife. It happened during what is commonly called an out-of-body experience. He was happy and peaceful on the Other Side, but he was determined to send a message of love to his family—especially to his mother. When her profound grief temporarily blocked the signs he sent, he essentially scouted around for someone to pass along the message. I was no more than a go-between.

Bobby showed me a few of his past lives so that I would better understand the next life he was planning. Both here and in his soul-planning session, words were used that might seem particularly outdated. For example, we'll see a past life in Victorian times in which some people were described as "lunatics" and "drunkards." At another point, Bobby's guide refers to "the disabled." Today, of course, we would say "a person with a mental illness," "an alcoholic," and "a person living with a disability" respectively. Other times, the way the guides speak seems a little stilted. It is important to me that these words be reported as remembered.

In recounting the Visit, I'll explore the idea of soul planning, as Bobby shared his planning session with me. We will look at how he designed potential challenges in his next life, and how he ultimately decided not to be born this time, leading his mother to endure a miscarriage. Bobby showed me how we might design our life lessons while retaining free will. We'll consider some of our entry points (for example, the family we choose to join) and, in keeping with divine balance, our exit points (from road accidents to illness and beyond).

As I raise the possibility that we plan our life challenges in advance, I appreciate our imaginations can take us to gruesome and graphic scenarios that dominate headlines and sear themselves into our collective thoughts—violence, kidnappings, natural disasters, and oppression among them. What's more, I fully respect there are many of you for whom no such imagination is necessary. You *live* with these experiences and their aftermath. Please be assured I present the following pages in good faith, with no intent to be cavalier about something that has made an enormous impact on your life. I willingly concede that no one person or school of thought can know or accommodate every spiritual possibility. I don't believe for a moment that my experience made me an expert on the Other Side. It did, however, give me startling insights I did not have before, and I'm propelled to share them.

Thank you for understanding that any spiritual experience is going to be subjective. As the book took shape, I was aware of the need both to qualify an idea as my personal belief and to avoid overuse of the phrase "I believe . . . ," which would be tedious to read again and again. I appreciate that what I'm about to share with you cannot be entered as "Exhibit A" or proved in a court of law. It cannot be measured, weighed, or photographed.

No doctor has ever biopsied a soul.

No scientist has ever studied one under a microscope.

No photographer has captured its essence under soft lighting or harsh glare.

Yet our souls are there, waiting patiently for us to become attuned.

NOTE: IF ANY OF THE CONTENT IN THIS BOOK RAISES PAINFUL ISSUES FOR YOU, PLEASE CONTACT A THERAPIST OR AN EMERGENCY HOTLINE.

# INTRODUCTION

This is not the book I set out to write; it is the one I feel compelled to share.

I don't say that from a point of ego, but from a place of service. I offer this experience for the comfort I am told it brings others.

You see, I'd initially planned a book on a different topic altogether (and let me add, my previous books are far more light-hearted).

Yet even as I began to outline that other title, something else kept gently nudging its way in: an experience I had some years ago. I resisted; it persisted.

I was reluctant to put my name to even a *light* spiritual book. As a journalist, I had always kept my faith and work separate. I was trained to report a news story in such a way that you as a reader, viewer, or listener could take it on its merits; my personal opinions were deliberately sidelined.

I tied myself in knots trying to preserve my privacy in writing this book, as I was certain it would finish my career in journalism. (It still might.) Write it as fiction, some suggested. I tried to adopt this approach in the hope it would roll off my tongue; I made some progress. Use a pseudonym, others advised. But maintaining anonymity is more difficult to achieve in our digital age. I also considered saying it was "based on a true story." No, that didn't feel quite right either. Finally, I decided to own it.

I had been mulling these options when I overheard snippets of a conversation in a park. A woman was venting to a friend, clearly hurting about something or someone in her life. She spat out that she felt cursed, that life "had it in" for her. The other person offered, "Everything happens for a reason."

It's a well-worn phrase you've heard and likely used. Perhaps it makes you roll your eyes or want to release a primal scream.

Yes, I thought. Things do happen for a reason—but perhaps not in the way the friend had intended. What if a family crisis, a terminal diagnosis, or a sudden job loss is not happening to us in a doomed or vengeful way, but rather happening by our own design? I don't mean only the painful episodes, but *especially* the painful ones—most often for our own growth, but sometimes for someone else's spiritual development. Through a choice *we* made. Might it comfort the lady if at some point she had considered she wasn't cursed, but instead was a powerful soul who had designed a life brimming in learning opportunities, including the very one causing her such heartache in that moment? Might that shift her mindset from victim to architect of her own life? Would it make her current circumstances a little easier to navigate? Would she feel a shift to a more proactive mindset if she knew she was holding the reins?

Allow me to share the essence of what I experienced.

My friend Jane and I had grown up together, sharing the adventures of childhood and the giddiness of adolescence. We had drifted in later years as life took us in different directions, when a seemingly chance meeting reignited our bond.

As we caught up on the intervening years, Jane shared that she had lost her third baby before he was born.

As anyone would, I offered all the support I could. At the same time, I knew there was really nothing anyone could say or do to ease her raw grief.

Some months later, her unborn baby, Bobby, visited me.

More specifically, his spirit took me on a brief tour of the Other Side. He had been sending his mother messages of love and comfort, but her grief temporarily blinded her to these signs. He looked around for someone or something to act as a go-between. It could have been anyone.

Her young son showed me his soul-planning session, when he planned his upcoming life with Jane and her husband, Joe. It included significant intellectual and physical challenges.

In the end, this little one decided not to come this time around. Jane miscarried.

However, her son was determined to convey a message of love to his parents from the Other Side.

That's the moment the experience began.

You'll see the book is divided into several parts. At its core is Bobby's Visit.

Rather than presenting the Visit in one, uninterrupted flow, which might be overwhelming or confusing without any explanation along the way, I will instead hit the pause button now and then on the narration. I want to give you an unrushed sense of how things unfolded and to explain more about what I was thinking at the time (or how I reflected on it later).

Given that many of you might be unfamiliar with soul planning, Part III includes a simple road map in case you would like a basic lay of the land. Finally, in Part IV, I share what happened after the Visit: the immediate aftermath of telling Bobby's parents and the longer-term impact it has had on me in the years since.

If you believe we go somewhere after we die, what do you call it? Heaven, the Other Side, Home, and the Afterlife are some of the terms commonly used. They all work for me, but I can't assume they work for you. I hope you'll bear with me as I draw on each of these at various times. Whatever the word, I'm referring to the same destination, whether you consider that a state of mind or an actual place.

Also, thank you for understanding why I've the changed the names of my friends.

# PART I

## Setting the Scene

*Chapter One*

# LIVING IN TWO WORLDS

In case we're meeting for the first time, I'd like to share something about myself. This is a personal book, so a little context might be useful.

I've long had a foot in two camps.

I come from a large family of first-generation immigrants, and we always felt the cultural pulls of India and Australia. One sister passed away in infancy. I never met Marian, but her brief visit continues to echo in our family (more on that later). All my older siblings were born in India; my younger sister and I arrived after the family moved to Australia. Our upbringing was happy and typical of its time. As children, we played outside with little supervision until it got dark. As teenagers, we blared pop music that frayed our parents' nerves. And we had all the usual crushes on classmates and movie stars alike.

We were raised as garden-variety Catholics, but a branch of the family is Hindu; that influence also left its imprint. Looking back, I believe it made me more open to the idea of past lives and rebirth. By contrast, Christian tradition teaches that we each have one lifetime on earth. To me, a loving God gives us more than one chance to get things right. I believe we have the chance to come here once, repeatedly, or not at all (in which case we would evolve, slowly but surely, through heavenly realms).

I spent time in India some years ago, working by day with Hindus and living by night with Catholic nuns in a convent. Christian references such as All Saints' Day or Communion mingled in conversation with *guru* and *Samsara*. You might be more familiar with the word *guru*, a Sanskrit term referring to a dispeller of darkness and seeker of light. I'm willing to bet it slipped into common Western usage after the Beatles traveled to India in the 1960s. Today, we speak of finance gurus, design gurus, and fashion gurus as shorthand for masters revered in their fields. *Samsara* refers to the cycle of rebirth and is found in both Hinduism and Buddhism. While the idea of rebirth might sound New Age or shocking to you, it is actually an ancient, common belief to more than a billion people.

Economically, our family experienced vastly different climates in each country. In Kolkata (then Calcutta), we had domestic staff, as a quarter billion Indians still have today. There was someone to cook, several women to look after the children, and another to sweep the floors and do the laundry. When my parents decided to move to Australia, they willingly surrendered this lifestyle to take on long jobs and to battle financially so that we children might have better opportunities.

In Australia, my father worked for the civil service, where he grappled on and off with racism (but where he also made firm friends). Later in life, he took a job as a janitor. My mother prepared meals in an industrial hospital kitchen. Money was tight, especially during the early years in a new country. Still, I was taken aback as a preteen when I overheard my older siblings reminiscing, "Do you remember that time we had ice cream?" I had to assume it was a luxury. My younger sister and I had an easier time of things simply by coming along when the family was more established.

College beckoned, and I delved into a degree in social work. The jobs that followed exposed me to a wide range of human experience, from family violence to various addictions and psychiatric illness. I witnessed sharply dysfunctional dynamics and how different personalities coped. Some battled on and then one day gave up, crumbling under the weight of abuse, limited work opportunities, or other challenges. But I also saw those who rose above it and became who they were supposed to be, not because of the circumstances they had been born into, but despite them. Without wishing those trials on them for a moment, I can see how it shaped the men and women they became. It was a grueling, gritty caseload to manage, let alone to live.

I married in my twenties, and I smile to think my husband and I could not have been more mismatched on paper. Jon is a scientist, a surfer, and an atheist. He embraces exercise at almost every level. I love the beach but prefer to walk along it rather than dipping in. God and I talk every day. (I'm mostly positive and grateful, though at times I sound like a disgruntled diner in a restaurant. *This is not the life I ordered!*) And while I enjoy a scenic hike, I usually need the lure of brunch at the end to keep trekking.

Later, I returned to university and graduated as a broadcast journalist. I started in local television news. A few years in, Jon was transferred overseas and so began sixteen years of living abroad. We hopscotched through half a dozen countries, including Russia, Chile, England, and the US. We recently moved back to Australia. Even now, I feel the tug of being in two worlds. I am proudly *from* Australia, but not always *of* Australia.

Somewhere along the way, I became an egg donor to two separate couples. Each were good friends in different phases of their fertility journeys. While I am a biological mother in the sense that the children carry my DNA, I am not a mother in any other way. This was another channel through which dual worlds played out. Later in the book we'll explore soul contracts: agreements made between souls for mutual growth. For now, let me say that I believe I made soul contracts with my friends to help them if they needed it. Once here on earth, I retained free will—as did they—on whether to follow through with this backup plan.

This ambiguity of having a foot in two camps continues to surface for me in various parts of my life. But far from feeling lost, I feel I've been given passports to two worlds. It also drew me to volunteer at a hospice, caring for those also on the brink of two realms, the physical and the spiritual. The chance to offer a little comfort to someone during the final weeks or days of their transition was a genuine honor.

*Chapter Two*

# EARLIER SPIRITUAL EXPERIENCES

I'd like to share a few events that gave me a framework by which to both welcome and better understand Bobby's Visit.

As this manuscript took shape, I pored over old diaries, emails, and other correspondence. In them, I found a tapestry of experiences that I had previously viewed in isolation. When looking at the bigger picture, I could see how each episode was interwoven with a previous one, even if they occurred years apart.

Let me say, I have no psychic ability whatsoever. I cannot foresee anything for myself or others. Nor do I have any formal training in theology. I enjoy reading light texts on different religions and their various traditions, but I have not extensively studied any of them. I often reflect on spirituality, turning over ideas in my head. Yet I don't question what for me are core tenets: the Other Side, the existence of angels and guides, and a loving God. They simply resonate. I defend your right to question, though. You're also welcome to read this as a work of fiction if that feels more comfortable. I am not seeking to convert anyone here; I am inviting you to take a journey with me. I believe (hope) it might bring you comfort and reassurance.

Given, then, that I have no psychic gifts or formal training, the experiences I'm about to share seem even more startling. If they can happen to me, clearly they can happen to anyone. I offer them as the context that helped me be more accepting of Bobby's Visit when it did occur.

## AGE SEVEN: A PREMONITION OF MY DEATH

I was in second grade, and it was my turn to read in front of the class. I adored my teacher, Miss T. I mispronounced "mayor," and she gently corrected me: "No, darling. This is how you say it." Far from feeling admonished, I felt a burst of love for Miss T.—to my child's mind, she wanted me to be the best reader ever.

Then, everything stopped. In front of me, I saw a woman with dark brown, shoulder-length hair. Her back was turned, yet I knew she was me as a grown-up. Next, I heard a loud crack to my left and saw this woman shot to the back of her head. I took this in passively, as if it were a movie. Then, a calm voice said softly,

> It will be violent,
> but it will be short,
> and then I'll take you Home.

I was not scared by what I saw, nor alarmed at what I heard; I trusted this voice completely. To me, it was a loving, protective angel. Today, I consider this shooting a potential exit point: a possible moment at which my death could occur, planned by me before I was born.

I did not think about this experience for many years afterward. It returned to me in my twenties (while listening to a band in a bar, no less) and registered an immediate and lasting impact. A long-buried truth had been remembered: death was not something to be feared. Nor would I be alone when the time came. I recalled the voice that was so still and spoke with such loving authority when it assured me I would be escorted back. I did not question it; I trusted it as a child would trust her mother or father. Remembering it as an adult brought the same reassurance.

## MY LATE TWENTIES: AN EXIT POINT IN AFRICA

Fast forward to a long-planned trip on a shoestring budget. We were white-water rafting with other tourists in Zimbabwe. Despite feeling terrified, I had allowed myself to be talked into it. Photos show Jon relaxed and reveling in the experience; I am frozen in fear.

We approached a severe rapid, the water violent. The next moment, I found myself flying overboard. Within seconds, my helmet peeled off, and the raft seemed miles away. My body and spirit were in direct contrast—my limbs were flailing desperately, yet my mind was calm, and I found myself thinking, "This is it. This is how it ends."

I was eventually spat into "calmer" rapids, though the current was still thrashing. Later, I was rescued by another group of rafters.

Again, this experience underscored for me that we choose a variety of circumstances—and ages—in which to depart this current life. This brush with death prompted me to reflect on my life's purpose.

## MY EARLY THIRTIES: UNDER ANESTHESIA

As mentioned, I've twice been an egg donor. During the second procedure in which the eggs were harvested, I had an unexpected visitor. A sweet, plump old lady stayed by my side throughout. I felt the softness of her pudgy hand in mine. She carried an air of joyful calm, telling me this was sure to be successful and that a baby boy was on his way.

When I woke up in recovery, my friend Kate (the egg recipient) was waiting. I asked the nurse to get the lady who had attended me so that I could thank her. The nurse seemed baffled, but when I insisted, she agreed to ask the other staff. She returned, saying no one by that description had been in the operating theater. When

I told them the lady's name, an ethnic nickname for "grandma," Kate blanched; it was the name she had called her own Eastern European grandmother. The egg donation was a success, and in time our friends welcomed a baby boy.

Being under anesthesia is a medically induced, altered state between life and death. This experience is significant for me because it is from this state that I believe many people choose an exit point. It's a portal through which a soul can choose to depart this life, deciding they have learned all they wish to learn this time around while undergoing a seemingly routine procedure. To the patient's shocked and grief-stricken family, the death could be extremely hard to fathom. Yet to the soul concerned, it could prove both a convenient "out" and a catalyst to growth for their loved ones in the aftermath of their loss.

This experience stunned me, as it did my friend. But as time progressed, I mentally filed it away. When I began to explore soul planning more, it returned to mind with a jolt. How did the elderly woman know what the procedure was for? How did she know a baby was coming—and a little boy, at that? Today, I consider this kind visitor and the baby himself part of the same soul group. I believe they both saw the heartache and anxiety around Kate, and how much she and her husband yearned for parenthood. Their message was one of love and reassurance.

## SHOWN MY SISTER'S EXIT POINT

In college, I drove a car that cost me four hundred dollars. A clunker, sure, but I had always felt safe in it.

One night, my brakes failed as I was driving my sister home. I pulled desperately on the hand brake, to no avail. We began to careen down a hill and gather speed. A park stretched out before us, and I imagined plowing into the sturdy wooden posts that encircled it. I dragged on the steering wheel to turn left, and thankfully the car didn't roll over as I half expected.

That was decades ago. Recently, this memory was replayed to me in vivid detail, but from a starkly different angle.

I was driving, and a series of pictures appeared in front of me, almost on my windshield. The images were gauzy and see-through; they didn't block my view of the road. I pulled aside.

I was shown that the braking incident had been a possible exit point (potential death) for my sister. She was around nineteen years old when this happened. The images revealed that she *chose* not to die at that moment. In turn, there was no accident and no fatality.

However, I was still walked through the repercussions of her death. This was a potential lesson planned not as punishment for me, but to present a set of circumstances through which I could learn a little or a lot. The choice remained mine. In the scenes that were laid out, I lost my way after the accident, and devoid of purpose, I began to drink. Heavily. Often. And alone. Her death—and my role in it—weighed greatly on me. A sense of worthlessness settled deep in my bones.

I was also shown ripple effects of this potential outcome. I saw in this "film" that while most of my immediate family were supportive after the accident, others tried but struggled to come to terms with her loss. They appeared to say and do the right things but harbored anger and palpable resentment toward me. My mother was one of them. I felt their rejection, and while given the chance to rise above it, I saw that I would have both flailed and failed. Miserably. I saw no images of having a husband or partner with whom to share my life and retreated further inward.

As soon as the pictures receded, I collected myself and called my sister. I had to hear her voice; it grounded me. My account of the experience must have been shocking, but she took it remarkably well. She kept saying gently, "But it didn't happen," and eventually that registered.

For days, I could think of nothing else, digesting the horror of possibly killing her, snuffing out her life before she had barely finished her teens. I wondered how my parents would have coped with losing another daughter (in addition to losing Marian the day she was born). I turned over in my head all the possibilities of how different my own life might have been. How could I have kept going, knowing I had killed her? I thought of the joys I would have robbed her of: backpacking, falling in love, a wedding day, children. And what about the long arm of the law? Would I have been jailed for manslaughter? Who would have employed me with a criminal record? Would I ever have married? Like aftershocks that follow an earthquake, shudders kept coming, rattling my body and my peace of mind.

Of all the ways I might have coped (or *not* coped) I was startled to see alcohol appear as a crutch because I am basically a teetotaler. I have never been drunk. I say that with neither pride nor embarrassment. While we always have wine on hand for friends, I never seemed to develop a taste myself.

The experience also recalled an odd reaction I'd had to alcohol some years before. One wintry evening, I'd gone to bed early to immerse myself in a new book. Jon came upstairs later and mentioned in passing he'd had two gin and tonics while watching a movie. Normally, I'd simply be amused by that, as it was rare. But my reaction was unsettling. I marched downstairs and poured the entire bottle of gin down the drain. Even as I did, I could feel how absurd it was, but I was propelled to continue. My family had no direct experience with alcoholism that might have triggered my response. Today, I believe I had some distant memory of that soul-planned blueprint when I might have turned to alcohol to cope with the specter of causing my sister's death.

As I look back on the car accident I was shown, I see its purpose. I realize now that my sister had made a soul contract with me—not only willingly, but even joyfully, before either of us were born. She chose one of her exit points from this life to potentially be a crucial intersection in my own life. She was giving me—*gifting* me—a life lesson brimming in opportunities for soul growth.

At the crucial point, she chose to stay—thank God. But in that moment, she also recognized that she had more of her own soul plan to fulfill—to travel, to study, and to embrace both marriage and motherhood. In turn, she honored soul contracts with her future husband and child.

# PART II

The Visit

## Chapter Three

# MEETING BOBBY

We were based in Houston and had just moved. In fact, it was possibly the shortest relocation on record. After a mix-up with our lease renewal, our apartment was inadvertently rented to others. The couple could not be persuaded to move next door— even with an identical floor plan! In the end, we moved thirty feet down the hall. Really.

Surrounded by boxes, I welcomed the chance to take a break from unpacking. I curled up on the sofa and began reading. It was mid-afternoon, and the sun shone meekly through the window.

Suddenly, I found myself on a beach.

I cannot tell you how I got there. I was simply transported. It happened as easily as glancing out a window of a train and noticing that my view had changed.

> The shore was to my left, the sky aglow with a beautiful sunset of pinks and oranges. To my right were sand dunes, majestic and a soft, creamy white. I looked down to see I was wearing a white tunic. I saw the grainy sand beneath me, but I'm not sure I felt it between my toes.

I took in this beautiful scene for a moment, then realized, "I need a hat!" [My skin is sprinkled with hyperpigmentation, known as chloasma, so I must avoid the sun.] Just as this thought crossed my mind, I felt a gentle tug on my tunic. I looked down to see a little boy of four or five years old, smiling so beautifully, so lovingly. With a quiet knowing, I realized he was the son of my close friend Jane, the baby she had recently lost in pregnancy. In some way, this made complete sense, yet we had never met.

As if to read my mind, he said, "We don't have chloasma here."

I laughed and replied, "That's a big word for a little boy."

"What age would you prefer I be? What age would you be more comfortable with?" He reminded me of his older brother, but he more strongly resembled his father, Joe, with a slightly longer and thinner face.

As he made this offer, he changed, morphing right before me. He grew from a little boy to a slightly older child and then to a preteen. He became a lanky teenager and filled out, as young men do. He was now taller than his dad and eventually became a wizened old man with salt in his beard. I didn't speak, but somehow he knew I wanted the little boy to return.

He became so, seemingly by thinking it. He nodded toward the sand dunes to our right, which became a movie screen onto which images were projected.

He was about to share something wondrous.

## REFLECTIONS

There was no buildup to my arrival on the Other Side—no tunnel and no light. Nor was it a near-death experience. My ears didn't pop the way they do at high altitude. And yet I was in a different dimension. I was simply and suddenly *there*. I felt enveloped in tranquility. I wasn't concerned with any element of my day back on earth; whether I'd unpacked something important or filed it away for safe keeping.

It was a simple, natural scene at the beach. I believe Bobby appeared to me as a little boy in order to feel welcoming and non-threatening. It reminds me that all major faiths feature angels as their messengers and the first message is, "Fear not!" They seek to reassure, to comfort.

Why a beach? I don't know, except that it seemed familiar and soothing. In that way, it served for me as, say, meadows do for other people's spiritual experiences. Had it been a different setting, I might have felt confused or disoriented.

I do not recall a direct light source such as the sun. We were surrounded by a lovely white light. The sunset colors were the only change to that. I wonder now if the colors were for my benefit because there was no sun to "set." On earth, a sunset signals the end of a day, yet time was not a factor here. I do not recall a breeze, nor feeling slightly cold or slightly warm. I was comfortable. Logic seeped in when I reached for a hat automatically. I wish I had thought to look back at the sofa, but I didn't.

I'm not sure how I knew the little boy was Jane's son, only that in that moment, it made complete sense. When he offered to change age, it was a kindness. He knew that I preferred to see him as a small boy, though I did not speak those words out loud. Our communication was by thought.

I believe your loved ones will do the same for you. Perhaps you have lost a child, and you worry that you won't be able to recognize your baby or toddler when you arrive on the Other Side. Your soul and theirs will communicate, joyfully, and they will know how best to present themselves to you.

The images on the sand dunes "screen" seemed to unfold in rapid fire, yet I could take them in easily. Bobby showed me several past lives with his present-day parents, Jane and Joe.

## A PAST LIFE SHARED BY BOBBY AND JANE

We saw a cheerfully loud dinner scene with a large family around the table. Bobby and Jane were siblings. Heavy, ornate tapestries decorated the walls. I got the impression they lived in Italy. Jane was the youngest girl, and Bobby was the youngest of the family. As the last-born daughter, Jane was expected to remain a spinster and care for her parents in their dotage. She loved her mother and father but wouldn't hear any talk of such a dull and dutiful fate.

Jane was a beauty and a paramour to a powerful man. Eventually the two were discovered. The scandal that followed threatened to ruin the family. In order to restore their social standing, it was decided that Bobby would be dispatched to the seminary.

This brother and sister were close. Jane was seven years older and fussed over Bobby, singing to him and generally coddling him like a second mother. When he was younger, he had loved his big sister creating songs and comic rhymes to entertain him.

Bobby reassured Jane that he wanted to go to the seminary and that she should remember this; he was not paying for the sins of a love affair. It was a harmonious situation, as Bobby was drawn to a life in the clergy but had been too timid to tell anyone. Having it unfold this way both helped him and publicly ushered in healing. Far from being a punishment, it was a moment of spiritual synchronicity.

# REFLECTIONS

I believe Bobby began to show me his past lives so that I would better understand the deep connection he has with his parents.

This scene was delightful on several levels: first for the celebration at hand, and second for the history and abiding affection that resonated between Bobby and his then-sister Jane (his mother in this present life). Far from being a monotonous routine, family life seemed a source of genuine pleasure for each of these souls, rich in texture and purpose.

The idea that Jane was involved in an extramarital affair was presented by Bobby with neutrality. It simply was. In viewing the scene, Bobby gave no signal he judged anyone, even as they were swept up in events and held strong opinions. The way in which the scandal was resolved by the "characters" on-screen was seen as predictable for its time. The synchronicity came in how it unfolded, giving Bobby a chance to follow his dream while helping the family restore honor. A two-for-one. This underscores for me how interconnected we are when we choose our soul plans. Both our plans and potential outcomes overlap with purpose.

Bobby adored Jane singing to him as a child. Jane's melodies were a loving sign of comfort and connection. It was their "thing." Soon, we'll see his reaction to the idea of experiencing deafness in his upcoming life. This small but pivotal detail shows how we choose not only relationships, but facets within those relationships in our next lives.

In viewing the scene, I did not find language to be a barrier. I'm not sure if the people on-screen spoke Italian and I somehow understood, or if it was translated so seamlessly that I didn't notice. (Despite having a fabulous Italian teacher in high school, I showed no aptitude beyond counting and basic greetings.) I've thought about this a lot since, because I believe we design lives across diverse cultures and countries. We presumably speak different languages given the circumstances we choose.

I later realized that my vision was perfect on the Other Side. I usually wear glasses or contact lenses for shortsightedness.

## A PAST LIFE SHARED BY BOBBY AND JOE

In the next images, Joe and Bobby were farmhands on neighboring properties. Bobby was only slightly younger, but he idolized Joe. He wanted to plow as Joe did, harvest as he did, milk the cows as he did. Bobby even longed to grow callouses on his hands like his "big brother."

A battle was brewing and talk of it dominated daily conversation. Bobby and Joe hatched a plan to run away and enlist, eager to leave behind rural life. They lied about their ages, determined not to miss out on the action. Joe had always protected Bobby, but during the fighting, Joe was injured, and it was Bobby who helped him to safety.

Standing beside me, Bobby said, "Remind my father [Joe] that he has spent many lives as a religious man; he will find this amusing" [as he is an atheist today]. We were then shown scenes in quick succession: Joe adhering to pagan rituals, later worshipping as a Buddhist, and another time living a life of quiet contemplation by the sea. We also glimpsed his days as an Orthodox Jew, wearing his hair long and curly at each side of his beard [sidelocks, or peyot], and participating in the ritualistic swaying in prayer.

## REFLECTIONS

This past life on the farm showed me the different roles we can choose to play among our soul group; there was a bond between Bobby and Joe, to be sure, but through friendship rather than familial lines this time around. Bobby showed me a caring dynamic between the boys, off on an adventure.

It also showed me that our relationships are chosen for what they can teach us; far beyond the practicalities of farming, there were moments that heralded Bobby's coming of age. And in a sense, he reversed roles to become Joe's rescuer on the battlefield. He became the caregiver, mirroring the role of guardian and protector his father would have assumed in this present life.

I smile to think of the diverse faiths Joe adopted during various lives. Over the centuries, he drew comfort and guidance from a framework offered by traditional organized religion, with its attendant rituals and codes of conduct. Today, he is an atheist. He has chosen to arrive this time without the internal experience and external support that faith provides so many people. It gives me pause to think of the scorn or outright contempt atheists endure today—likely by souls who themselves have been atheists in previous lives.

Some elements of this particular past life seemed vaguely familiar. I have scoured books and blogs and searched extensively online but cannot locate anything that resembles this experience. If it seems familiar to you, please contact me. Nonetheless, I offer it here in good faith, as it was shown to me.

### A FEW OF BOBBY'S OTHER LIVES

Having shared images of past lives with Jane and Joe [his mother and father in this life], Bobby then showed me some of his other incarnations.

He was an academic in Asia hundreds of years ago. He was entrusted to prepare special documents, sometimes in other languages, for trade deals—spices, I think—and wider negotiations. These were overseen by a ruling party or family, and they were well pleased [the expression used at the time] with his efforts.

Another scene followed in what appeared to be Victorian times. In his youth, Bobby would pass an almshouse [a poorhouse] each day on his way to school. Eventually, he summoned the courage to go in, and witnessed people in pushchairs [wheelchairs], along with lunatics and drunkards [to use the language of the day], passing their days in squalor. Bobby eventually befriended a blind girl named Annie. He would read aloud, taking delight in painting imaginary worlds for her. He was discouraged from going, as he was from a good family. Bobby learned to soak rags and to tie Annie's hair so that she could have curls in the morning. He was widely ridiculed for that; this was women's work, all of it. Through his past lives, Bobby retained a deep wellspring of compassion. He even lobbied for better quality food for those who lived in the almshouse, and he sometimes secured fresh vegetables and fruit for the residents, which they talked about long after. Prior to this, they endured endless bowls of thin gruel.

Later, the setting changed to a stiflingly hot and dry climate, where sandstorms swept the plains. Bobby played with a boy whose family squatted on the rooftop of the building in which he lived. When he was older, Bobby became an activist, leading protests to shine a light on the deplorable living conditions of the poor in his homeland.

## REFLECTIONS

I found this medley of past lives both riveting and revealing. Bobby chose to be born into vastly different time periods and social classes. He moved from being an accomplished older academic, to a caring young man (who defied his parents to visit the almshouse), to a boy who played on his rooftop with other children. He embraced a wide range of lifestyles, daily routines, and identities.

The common thread throughout is Bobby's caring nature and generosity of spirit. We may adopt dramatically different roles, but I believe we retain our core essence. I see a connection with Jane and Joe, who are breathtakingly generous people. I have witnessed how their gifts ease significant hardships and transform lives. I do not say that lightly. I have to think that this was one of the qualities that made Bobby gravitate to these souls as his parents.

I believe each of these three souls has known poverty in other lives, and not only overcome it, but seen how money can be used for good—to provide opportunity and security, and to remove despair. To paraphrase P. T. Barnum, money is a terrible master but a wonderful servant.

We all have a relationship to money, and we can approach it from a point of scarcity (worrying there will never be enough) or from a point of abundance (having faith that our needs will be not only met but exceeded).

Not knowing the security of abundance, some hold on to money ever tighter after experiencing poverty. I recall a celebrity interview in which an actress declared, "I'll never be poor again." She demanded exorbitant appearance fees, even for charity galas—I believe now that she clung to a cellular memory of poverty, imprinted by her past lives.

*Chapter Four*

# BOBBY'S SOUL-PLANNING SESSION

N ext, Bobby nodded toward our left. The beach was now replaced with a white room, a soft white that didn't hurt my eyes. A few dozen people were seated in a circle, extending several rows out. Everyone wore white tunics, but their garments were made of light rather than the cloth I wore. I recognized this scene from reading about the Other Side and began to exclaim, "Oh my God, I know this . . . ," except it came out as, "Oh my, I know this . . ."

Bobby smiled cheekily and said, "We don't use that word [God] in that way."

In the next moment, Bobby was no longer by my side. He stood in the middle of the circle and now adopted the look of a young adult, though still plainly recognizable. He was joined by his spirit guides and guardian angels. The atmosphere was infused with tremendous love and support.

I said, "Wait. I've read about this. How do I know that I'm not just imagining it?"

He gently admonished me to look into my soul and to trust it. He added: "You read not to discover, but to remember."  ←

# REFLECTIONS

I believe Bobby was saying here that the Other Side is our real Home, and when we arrive on earth, we need to temporarily forget where we came from and the soul plan we have made. When we move from the Other Side to the earthly realm, we pass through the Veil of Forgetfulness, also known as simply the Veil. This represents the border between the physical and spiritual worlds. Our memories of our higher selves and our divine gifts dissolve; we must learn to meet our goals without benefit of either.

This scene, where the souls gather, shook me to my core. Yet it instilled in me a sense of wonder, as though suddenly recalling a joyous, long-buried childhood memory and being able to relish it afresh. My reaction—my recognition of this scene—registered powerfully. The feeling was one of deep familiarity, something I believe lies in us all. Even when Bobby gently admonished me, there was no actual judgment. Judgment is a feature of earthly life.

I was neither startled nor curious when Bobby appeared in one moment as a child and the next as a young man in the center of his soul-planning session. This transformation was presented as seemingly routine, so I accepted it as such. It was as though he was simply changing costumes.

If one or more of Bobby's guides were deceased relatives, I did not recognize them. Still, the connection among them seemed to be one of trust, love, and respect. They wanted the best for Bobby; he knew and appreciated this.

## BOBBY WEIGHS THE PLAN FOR HIS NEXT LIFE

This was not the first meeting on Bobby's upcoming lifetime. And yet no one felt any pressure to reach a conclusion. There was no sense of hurry or a rush to completion. Instead, the session began with reviewing the decisions already made. It was a chance to recap the foundation of the soul plan before adding another major element.

*thoughtful soul planning in great detail*

Bobby had been mulling his options for some time. Prior to this planning session, he had already chosen his parents, and they had chosen him. He had carefully considered their personalities and qualities for what they could teach him. Jane and Joe still attended these sessions for "updates" as Bobby's soul plan took shape and sat among those in the circle, waiting patiently to be called on.

Likewise, Bobby had chosen his siblings, who were also in agreement. In turn, I believe he would have attended their soul-planning sessions so that his lessons might better dovetail with their own. The members of this family unit formed the major basis for his identity. He also chose his gender, sexual orientation, ethnicity, and accordingly, his looks. His olive, European complexion, his brown eyes, his build, and other features were all conscious choices.

Having decided *whom* to live with, Bobby was now mulling *how* to live. He turned his attention to another critical component of his soul plan: whether he would choose to have a disability in this next life. He seemed to be wrestling with an inner push and pull. The guides and other souls acknowledged that for him to even consider such a challenge was a sign of an advanced soul. He could always opt, as all souls can, to never return to the earthly realm but to evolve, gently, on the Other Side itself, in the world of absolutes [where love exists unopposed] rather than the world of duality [where good/bad exist].

One guide said, "You have cared for the disabled [in your previous lives]. You have advocated for the disabled. Are you ready to be one of them?"

Bobby had been mulling over blindness, to honor Annie from his life in Victorian England, but ultimately it didn't feel quite right. [On the Other Side, I believe we have clarity of each past life, including whom we knew and the roles we played in each other's plans.]

Working through the earthly five senses, the guide suggested deafness instead. Bobby immediately dismissed this; he had adored Jane singing to him in a previous life and did not want to spend a lifetime with her in silence. He explored other options, confident that he could weigh alternatives—including the choice to simply not go through with this upcoming life.

While buoyed by the support he was receiving, Bobby still pondered this decision. Part of the job of the angels and spirit guides was to help infuse his soul plan with both a solid framework and finer detail. Their gentle but insightful questioning helped him plan the timing by which things would unfold. Would his main challenges be clumped together, more evenly spaced, or sprinkled throughout his life in some other way?

One guide asked, "What sort of disability do you have in mind?"

Bobby considered a mixture of learning opportunities for this upcoming incarnation. His main challenge would be an intellectual disability, with secondary physical disabilities. These, in turn, would spark educational, health, and social issues to traverse, both for Bobby and his parents. His selections became more specific, but his ambivalence about arriving remained.

The guide suggested calling on key players in Bobby's life to further explore his plan.

Bobby looked around the cluster that encircled him. He nodded and smiled in recognition at two individuals. Jane and Joe stood up and emerged from different parts of the room to the center of the circle. They smiled at each other and held hands. This was another chance to discuss, question, or reaffirm their involvement. Sometimes souls change their mind or elect to play a different role depending on the finer points of a lesson, the timing, or the intensity. They, too, have free will.

Bobby: Will you love me and guide me?

Jane and Joe: We will.

Bobby: The life I am planning is complex. It involves suffering and challenges.

Jane and Joe: We accept this, as it will aid your spiritual growth.

Bobby: I remain undecided. If I choose to forgo this incarnation [and to stay on the Other Side], you will be left awash in anguish and deep grief [because the pregnancy would end at Bobby's choosing. It had not been decided at what stage in the pregnancy this might occur. It might involve an early miscarriage or the delivery of a stillborn baby.]

Jane and Joe: We will honor your choice to return here [to the Other Side], and we will cope. [They accepted this possibility as an expression of Bobby's free will.]

The spirit guide gently intervened to provide context and insight.

Guide: Whether you stay or whether you return, your impact will be felt across many souls. Might you reconsider your birth order?

At that moment, another soul stood up. I recognized him instantly as Elliot, one of the twins born from Jane's first pregnancy. The other was a twin sister, who would likely harbor jealousy toward Bobby for the extra attention he would receive.

Elliot: Let me be born first. [Turning to Bobby] If you stay, I will be your fierce protector; if you decide not to go, [turning to Jane and Joe] you will have a healthy child.

Guide: We support this, but the choice remains yours. [Turning to Jane and Joe] You would know joy before heartache. You would know hope before despair.

[Allow me to state the obvious: This is not to imply that children with disabilities do not spark their own joy. Rather, it is to explain that Jane and Joe might first experience the tumult of parenthood without the additional element of having a child with special needs.]

There was further discussion which I couldn't hear. I didn't understand the fragmented bits I caught, except for a reference to equilibrium. I think this referred to a state of spiritual equilibrium, which I believe is a key component of the Other Side. I do not know why I was excluded from this. Perhaps there are parts of a soul-planning session that are private, and observers need not be privy to it.

The guide turned to Bobby's father with a loving face that reflected compassion and wisdom.

Guide: [To Joe] You have planned a lifetime without benefit of organized religion, as has served you well in prior incarnations. [If Bobby chooses not to go ahead] You will suffer deep loss without comforting rituals. Your grief will be undiluted.

Joe: I accept this as part of my journey.

The guide then spoke tenderly to Bobby's mother.

Guide: [To Jane] You have chosen a subset of your soul group [raised as Christian] this time whose religion strongly influences your daily life. You could suffer a crisis of faith, angry that God would seemingly send you this cross to bear. If you miscarry, that would be an acute loss in itself. If you are even momentarily relieved, you would feel shame and guilt. You could also be isolated as you might have fewer people to confide in without judgment.

Jane: I will undertake this risk, as doing so gives him [Bobby] the courage to contemplate this lifetime at all.

## REFLECTIONS

Bobby's spirit guides played their role, gently poking and prodding his thinking. They prompted him to consider his soul plan from many different angles while respecting his choices. I saw they drew on their own extensive catalog of firsthand human experience to pose questions about his upcoming life, helping him sift through his options.

The guides showed a loving duty of care toward Bobby's parents, and indeed to each soul participating in this soul plan. While it always remained Bobby's choice to be born, each soul chooses its circumstances. And each retains free will, both in this planning stage and while on earth. In turn, Bobby felt deep gratitude toward each of them for the roles they were taking on. When Elliot vowed to be Bobby's protector, Bobby seemed to swell with pride as if to say, "That's my big brother." It is a dynamic we have all seen in schoolyards and playgrounds.

I'd not considered birth order as something chosen at the soul level, yet with so much else planned and orchestrated, it makes sense to me. Siblings are never just siblings; our dynamics naturally change whether we are older/younger or brother/sister. We adopt—or are assigned—nicknames in our roles, such as the trailblazing firstborn or the baby in the family who is seemingly indulged well into adulthood. We might willingly play into these roles or spend our lives chafing against them; they all shape who we become. Consider behaviors such as "second-child syndrome" when a child feels their needs, milestones, or contributions fade in comparison to those of an elder sibling.

Jane shared that had she first become pregnant with Bobby, she and Joe would not have gone on to have more children. They would have considered the risk too high to have another child with a disability. This again speaks to the interconnection among souls. Would their twins (born prior to Bobby) have been born to someone else? Would those two souls have still arrived together?

And what of Jane and Joe's soul plans? How would they come to terms with this? Would they forever feel a gaping hole in their hearts? Or would they, in time, learn to embrace life as a couple rather than as a family?

## A SUPPORT CREW MAKES AN APPEARANCE

I watched with interest as two other people stood up.

The first was a young man, Mike. I recognized him from Bobby's extended family [in this present life]. Mike said that he was planning a similar life of overcoming obstacles, though with a much milder physical disability than Bobby was contemplating right now. He was here to offer his support to Bobby.

Also, I saw a woman whom I initially did not recognize. When our eyes met, though, I was pleasantly surprised to see she was Krishna, a friend of Jane's [in this present life]. Krishna was planning a life of significant loss, which featured no less than half a dozen miscarriages, ranging from several weeks into the pregnancy to almost full term. She offered to be a support to Jane. That said, Krishna hadn't yet decided on some elements of her own upcoming life. She reassured Jane they would meet—either as peers or later, with Krishna a much older woman. Either way, she would genuinely under-stand Jane's pain and loss and would prove a solid support.

## REFLECTIONS

With the appearance of Mike and Krishna, we're shown the strikingly loving way souls plan to arrive at the same time, for both growth and support. Some may play a fleeting role, appearing in our lives just long enough to lend a fresh perspec-tive or to help pivot us in a different direction. Others stay for the long haul. Both types involve soul contracts (agreements) made between people to aid each other's growth and fulfill their soul plans.

I was interested to note Mike's part in this. He would share a gender and the experience of disability with Bobby. While others might extend sympathy by their encouraging words or practical help, Mike could offer empathy. His experience would aid enormously.

We see here that Krishna had committed to meeting with Jane and to befriending her, but had not yet decided when; she was still designing her own soul plan. This highlights the flexibility we have to move around key elements of our upcoming lives. I believe if one of the women had veered off her path enough to prevent this meeting from happening, their guides would have helped orchestrate a fresh opportunity. In this way, the plan could still unfold while each woman retained her free will to engage.

Further, Krishna was planning a life of profound and repeated loss. A certain amount of loss is inevitable in life, including the passing of a loved one. But *half a dozen* miscarriages? I try to imagine the exhilaration of falling pregnant only to have to confront losing my unborn child. This would be devastating if it happened once, let alone time and again. Far from being an object of punishment or a source of pity, Krishna was an especially advanced soul to design such challenges. Her plan involved developing vast reserves of resilience to keep going and growing.

I was astounded at Krishna's wealth of emotional stamina and at the astonishing gift she offered repeatedly to these souls. By agreeing to be their mother and knowing the possibility that not one but many might likely choose not to be born, she was making a tremendous personal sacrifice so that they might have a choice. She repeatedly put their needs before her own. Krishna may not have held her babies, but her selflessness was the very essence of motherhood. I believe her soul will record and reflect tremendous spiritual growth after such harrowing experiences.

## BOBBY'S EXIT POINTS:
## WILLINGLY AND CREATIVELY DESIGNED

In this pre-birth planning session, there was divine balance, which I believe is the signature mark of the Other Side. Just as Bobby chose the manner and circumstances in which he would arrive, it equally made sense that he would choose options by which he would depart this upcoming life. After all, the journey we plan is a round trip, not one-way.

The guide asked Bobby what other potential departures he would like to build into his soul plan should he choose not to be born. Discussion followed as to other exit points in his early life: an accident involving a tricycle perhaps? Another soul, the one who would have caused this accident, stood up and demurred. He had been planning a theme of addiction involving alcohol abuse and potentially manifested in drunk driving. Still, he felt this would not complement his learning arc as well as he'd first hoped. I didn't recognize this man at all. Bobby accepted his decision. Another option was a diagnosis of childhood cancer by age twelve.

### REFLECTIONS

I was fascinated by these options. It's natural to ask why any soul would plan the potential for such painful challenges. I can only return to simple but central notions: we come here to learn, and we do not learn in situations of perfect harmony, perfect health, or consistently wise life choices. When we consider the breadth, depth, and variety of ways we can live and die as humans, we see the vast choices laid before us.

Bobby was offered multiple exit points to afford him more flexibility as to when and how he might depart this lifetime. The more variables, the more options he has in how his life might play out. He has free will in deciding when and how to call "time out."

consistently wise choices ⇒ no learning

Bobby's options further underscore our sheer interconnection: one soul's choice of exit point could spark extensive ramifications for the path another soul would walk in the aftermath of their loss.

If he were to navigate cancer in his early years or die an otherwise grueling death, what of the impact on his parents? Would one of them turn to alcohol, drugs, or another outlet to numb their pain? Would they grow apart or closer together? Would any subsequent children be born into a tighter union or a crumbling marriage rooted in despair? Would one or both suffer a crisis of faith or grow more resilient? And what of Bobby's siblings, extended family, friends, and neighbors? Would it spark a role in activism for one of them, say, pushing for tighter drunk-driving laws or fund-raising for awareness campaigns? Could their passion or life purpose be designed to spring directly from an exit point chosen by someone else?

*Chapter Five*

# UNEXPECTED NEWS

W e had seen Bobby weigh his options on his life challenges. Next, we moved ahead to observe episodes of
Jane and Joe's future lives on earth. Just as earlier we had
seen samples of their past lives, now we were looking into
the future. Time is fluid on the Other Side.

The spirit guide showed us that Jane and Joe had planned
to experience secondary infertility [an inability to conceive
after having had one or more children] before falling pregnant with Bobby. It was a significantly courageous and ardu-
ous challenge to adopt. The longer they craved another child,
the deeper their anguish and the more intricate the dilemma
they faced both individually and as a couple. In turn, the more
extensive would be their spiritual growth.

How would they reconcile the news of infertility with a
primal and loving desire to extend their family? The way
we choose to approach obstacles—to confront them, bury
them, deny them—all have an impact on the way our soul
evolves.

# REFLECTIONS

Individuals and couples suffering secondary infertility face less support than those who are confronting infertility for the first time. It's as if the world only has so much compassion to hand out; those who already have one child are told to be grateful and are shunted to the back of the line. Yet they simply ache to complete their families, to give their child a brother or sister.

Let's explore the issue of time.

It's often said that time is an earthly construct. We speak of the past, present, and future in a linear way. Our experiences of time are ordered, and we don't expect to hop from one dimension to another. My perception of the Other Side, though, was different. Just as Bobby could grow and mature before my eyes from a small boy to an elderly man, so, too, he could adopt a persona as he wished, simply by thought.

A simple comparison: think about a joyful pastime in which you immerse yourself. Time seems to "stop" for some people, while it "flies" for others. You might have heard of flow theory in psychology. Flow is said to be an altered mental state of focused immersion. It can also be said that at this moment, our soul is in harmony with our mind and body—there is synchronicity. By comparison, when we're involved in a painful or dull activity, time can seem to drag. Perception is reality.

Spiritual authors sometimes reference time as a spider web of sorts. This makes sense to me, as everything I experienced and witnessed in Bobby's Visit—be it access to past lives, current plans, or future events—was all happening in the "now."

## BOBBY WATCHES JANE AND JOE REACT TO THE PREGNANCY

Bobby saw his parents' joyful response to finally falling pregnant after enduring this agonizing time of secondary infertility. Jane and Joe naturally celebrated this news with family and friends.

In time, Bobby's soul was also present when Jane and Joe learned at a routine sonogram that their child would have a disability. There was utter devastation and raw grief at losing the dreams they held for this baby. There were also repercussions for what this meant for their immediate family. What would the future look like? What quality of life would their baby have? What would it mean for Bobby's siblings, especially after their parents had died? Would Jane and Joe be assigning the twins a lifelong responsibility? Would they become angry or resentful? What about wider health issues for Bobby beyond his main disability?

Bobby watched events unfold without judgment. He knew of the Veil, which all souls must pass through on the way to the physical plane, and the necessary memory loss of the Other Side. He saw his parents' deep heartache. He witnessed the tears and anguish washing over Jane at the sheer injustice of it all. He watched as they went back and forth, wrestling with how they would raise a child with a disability. He saw Jane's faith was sorely tested.

## REFLECTIONS

Bobby stayed close to his parents at all times, through both joyous news and devastation. He understood that they had passed the border between the spiritual and physical worlds, and that in doing so, they had forgotten the soul plans agreed to on the Other Side. Because of this, news of his disability (though he was yet an unborn child) was distressing for them.

As I think back on this experience, I am reminded that while our loved ones stay close, they do not do so passively. They actively take joy, feel pride, and wish to soothe our heartache. They send encouragement to keep us going through setbacks and celebrate our victories.

*Chapter Six*

# BOBBY MAKES HIS DECISION

B obby had framed a complex life, rich in opportunities for
the growth he sought. He had chosen members of his
family unit, and they had chosen him. The guide suggested,
lovingly and with nonjudgment, that perhaps he had over-
reached a little. It might be helpful to remember that as
we plan our upcoming lives, we do so in an atmosphere
of incomparable support. We are enthusiastic and bravely
optimistic. This can make a soul feel somewhat invincible.
"Bring it on," we seem to think, eager to take on the challenges of the world. We know that this upcoming life might
be only seven or eight decades (in earthly terms), if not
far shorter, so we can be willing to cram it full of learning
opportunities.

Bobby further reflected on how his life might play out.

He decided that this particular soul path was a life he was
not ready to experience at this moment.

*He chose not to be born.*

After all the soul searching, it was as simple—and as far
reaching—as that.

# REFLECTIONS

Bobby chose not to follow through with an earthly birth this time. He elected to physically exit via miscarriage. Of course, Jane would have to endure this tragedy to honor his choice. A seemingly straightforward decision by Bobby on whether or not to be born would set in motion powerful repercussions for his parents—especially Jane. As Bobby rendered his decision from the Other Side, Jane was left to bear the brunt of that result on earth. (I respect both parents felt the impact.) A crisis of faith could unfold: would Jane and Joe's sense of faith or fairness in life be tested and reclaimed, set aside, or abandoned altogether?

Jane would have had her own soul-planning sessions. I did not observe them in my time on the Other Side, but I draw basic conclusions from what I observed with Bobby.

This time around, Jane elected to join a subset of her wider soul group who were planning to share strong Christian values. I believe subsets choose to arrive at the same time, working through broader life themes together. She chose her own parents and European culture. She would be raised with staunch ideas around faith. She had to confront the possibility of her baby either not being born or else born with considerable disabilities. She willingly assumed this risk for the opportunity it would give Bobby to grow spiritually. His choice stemmed from *her* resolute pain. This strikes me as incredibly gracious and spiritually attuned of Jane.

She and Joe wrestled with gut-wrenching heartache and anger. Jane felt battered emotionally and spiritually. She prayed fervently for a healthier outcome for their child. While praying, any of us might plead, bargain, or demand. We struggle with the injustice of bad things happening to good people. The energy around these feelings can vary on any given day, for any person. Jane suffered acutely, mired in a crisis of faith.

I believe Jane's soul is spiritually evolved. She took on the weight of this challenge and anguish for Bobby's chance to arrive and grow. If he chose to be physically born, Jane would give birth to him and share that closest of bonds between mother and child.

Bobby's choice in coming or staying on the Other Side would spark heartache either way for Jane. If Bobby chose not to be born, she would plunge into grief and would need to reach deep within herself to move through that darkness. If he chose this life on earth, Jane would endure a difficult pregnancy. She would begin to grieve the hopes and dreams she and Joe had for their child before ever meeting him. Once he arrived, they would have to surmount the challenge of meeting his needs here on earth. All the while, they would have to (and want to) find the time and energy to be there for their twins.

## THE MISCARRIAGE

As the pregnancy progressed, more complications arose and, in keeping with Bobby's decision, his spirit left to return Home. Given the time that had now elapsed, Jane had to deliver Bobby as stillborn.

Here, we arrive at two central messages from Bobby. First, his soul departed the body before any physical procedure took place. He emphasized this to me as he sought to reassure his parents he did not suffer. I believe this occurs in any circumstance involving physical trauma, be it a miscarriage, a car accident, or a termination. Second, he sent a pivotal message of unconditional love and gratitude to his parents. Bobby saw that Jane and Joe honored his wishes at great personal and emotional cost.

Again, Bobby stressed that his soul departed his unborn body before his mother ever arrived at the hospital. He remained close by, and he described the tremendous, powerful love that resonated in that room. He recalled the souls who were there to accompany him Home. He sought to impress on Jane and Joe to remember and hold dear the peace that came: it was his love, to be sure, but just as powerfully it was gratitude, which has a sacred vibration of its own. His soul was—and is—so grateful for the tremendous courage Jane and Joe showed to honor his choice not to come this time.

## REFLECTIONS

There can surely be no greater pain than losing a child. It must be a depth of despair that drives a person to their breaking point, to question the world and the seeming inaction of a loving God to prevent it. The parents have lost not only their baby, but also the hopes and dreams for their loved one and the joy he or she would have brought their wider family.

I strongly believe that throughout the pregnancy, the heartache of the delivery, and its aftermath, Jane and Joe were surrounded by an enormous and powerful angelic army. Angels and spirit guides always seek to infuse a situation with compassion and love. I can only try to imagine the depths of despair that must have settled in Jane and Joe's hearts, but I know that angels were working, gently but resolutely, to usher in healing and spiritual equilibrium.

Jane shared that after she delivered Bobby, she and Joe were given private time with their baby. As they held and cherished their little boy, whispering to him how much he was loved, something extraordinary occurred. Jane noticed the room was overcome with light. "Did you see that?" she asked Joe, but he was lost in thought and grief. A sense of overwhelming peace came over Jane. It is only now, years later, that I realize this incident has the hallmarks of a "shared death experience" (discussed in more detail later). In essence, it is when a loved one's transition Home is felt by those present. And who closer than a mother to experience this?

Parents who lose a child become part of a club that anyone would dread to join. One day, long after the initial rawness (which I am not suggesting dissipates quickly), they might consider the possibility that this exit was something of their child's choosing (and equally, it is their right to dismiss this possibility). It might bring them comfort to know or remember that the soul sheds its physical body before severe pain and trauma. And to reflect on why their child might have chosen this exit point at all. What might the repercussions be? Viewing things from the standpoint of soul planning can help make sense out of seemingly senseless pain and loss.

*Chapter Seven*

# A GIFT:
# SHOWN A PAST LIFE OF MY OWN

This is the final part of the Visit that I recall.

The images on-screen changed once again, and I was surprised to see one of my own past lives unfold.

I was shown a lifetime where I was mired in poverty and had many children. I was grinding wheat for bread, life was grueling, and my husband and I were never sure how we would feed our brood. I was shown three of our children, all little, each coming down in turn with the consumption [tuberculosis]. Each time, I vowed my baby would recover. I bartered for ingredients in the village market to make a special broth I was convinced would help. Nothing did. And then my heart would break once again when I saw the telltale blood they coughed up on my sleeve or tunic as I nursed them.

Then came another twist: I had a sister, whom I loved dearly. She ached to be a mother, but she was barren [the word used at the time]. I didn't recognize her from this current life. My husband and I had given her our youngest child. As the disease spread through our village, this little boy survived, as he lived away from us. His survival came from the pain of giving him to another.

That little boy was Jon, my husband in this life. I recognized him immediately. We were connected [as birth mother and son] yet separated in that lifetime. We knew we'd be together again soon.

We moved forward in time. In the next scene, I was much older. I carried inside me much suffering at the loss of life in my family. Eventually, I endured a breakdown and suffered a stroke or heart attack. My death was quick, and I was Home in a moment. When I returned, I was calm but with memories of loss raw and fresh, I was adamant in my next few lives I would not be a mother. My guides supported this.

I asked Bobby if he and I had shared many lifetimes together. He said a few, but more peripherally. So why visit *me* to convey the message? Surely, he could have chosen someone or something else?

He said simply, "You are open to this."

He said he saw his parents' heartache and was determined to get a message through. He wanted Jane, Joe, and his siblings to remember he was close by and that he felt their ceaseless love for him and how they ached for him. Just as other souls had been there for Bobby as his soul departed earth, so, too, would he be there for them when their time came. He had sent his parents signs to comfort and reassure them, but grief had blinded them to his messages. Combined with an element of unwarranted guilt, it became even harder for them to stay attuned to signs of comfort.

## REFLECTIONS

I believe these images stemmed from my most recent past life.

This experience seemed to be offered as a thank-you for conveying Bobby's message. At least, that's the way I made sense of it. It might have been simply to better understand his own past lives.

With Bobby's past incarnations, I watched them as I would a movie: entranced, but in a passive way. This time, though, I almost became immersed in each scene. I felt like I could have stepped into that modest home with its dirt floor and felt the woman's hunger in my stomach, her fatigue in my bones, her despair in my heart. I could hear the bustle in the marketplace, the chatter, and the energy.

As I thought further, I realized that consumption was another name for tuberculosis (TB). In my twenties, I had spent a few months volunteering in India, first at a hospice and later at a leprosy hospital in the countryside. I cherished my time in each setting, but I remembered with a jolt that when I finished for the day with the leprosy patients, I would make my way to the TB ward. I was drawn to it, and I recall thinking early on that I should have requested to be rostered across both hospital wings. I believe now that inclination sprung from a faint memory of my past life as a mother who knew the devastation of that disease firsthand.

I felt elation but also shock that Jon had appeared as a prior connection. As I've mentioned, Jon and I chose not to have children in this present life, but I do have a biological son and daughter through my experience as an egg donor. I'm not sure what to make of fertility cropping up in both my past and present lives. Perhaps other women had helped me to become a mother, and this was my chance to give back.

While watching, I had imagined, or even half assumed, that Bobby and I must have been close for him to take me on this journey. Given the intimacy of the experience, surely we must have had a solid connection for him to trust me, I thought. In fact, it seems we are only part of a wider soul group. I was chosen because I was open to the experience rather than likely to mock it or dismiss it. I had to be only one of many who could have done the job, and it was simply my good fortune to be selected.

The way Bobby chose to convey his message sprang from a strong love of his present-day parents. He was determined to reach out to them to convey that love and reassurance. I believe he particularly sought to comfort Jane.

Equally, Bobby seemed quietly adamant that his family know that he stays near them. This reminds me: Jane shared that she was in bed one early morning soon after losing Bobby, in that twilight state between deep sleep and waking. She felt the unmistakable weight and wriggle of a little one, and assumed it was one of her twins who had crawled into bed. When she reached out, no one was there. I believe this is just one of the many ways Bobby made his presence felt, always with a message of love.

# Chapter Eight

## TELLING JANE AND JOE

I don't know how long the Visit took. Perhaps just minutes. Gradually, I sort of "came to." I arrived back in the same way— no tunnel, no light. It took a little while to reorient myself. It was a bit like waking up in an unfamiliar hotel room on your first day of vacation; you forget for an instant that you landed last night, and you need a moment to be grounded. I became aware of our apartment, feeling the sofa cushion beneath me and hearing the faint traffic in the street below.

I simply stared into space. I sat in silence and felt buffered from daily concerns.

I knew how odd this experience would sound. I knew how it would come across. But equally, I knew instinctively I had to share it with Jane and Joe. I couldn't know with certainty how they would receive it, but I had no right to keep this to myself.

They were living in another time zone, and I had to wait for a decent hour to phone them. The clock seemed to drag. While I intended to call my friends at a more reasonable time, I was bursting by 5:00 a.m. their side. I was excited but also apprehensive that I might forget the details of the experience before I could share them. I called and heard Jane's voice, groggy and heavy with sleep. I immediately asked her to put me on speaker phone; I wasn't sure I could relate the experience fully a second time. Joe listened politely, but later Jane went into another room, and we talked more.

Jane was open to the idea of signs from her little boy. She welcomed them, but we were both taken aback at the experience.

Afterward, I sat at my computer and poured pages onto the screen in minutes. The journalist in me had to record it while it was fresh, though it has remained so in my mind. At the time, though, I couldn't risk it, as I had nothing on that scale for comparison.

I sat lost in thought, knowing it was seared into me.

As grateful as I am for the experience, I would have preferred that it had happened to Jane. She had been through so much. She and Joe deserved to hear directly from Bobby. I believe when we're in the depths of grief, we can temporarily block signs from our loved ones. And even if we do notice signs, that same grief can sometimes cloud us with doubt.

Bobby had told me that I was simply someone who was open to the idea. But I still wonder why he came to me, thousands of miles from Jane and Joe, rather than someone in their hometown. Surely it would have been good for his mother to sit with the go-between to get more of a sense of things? I am reminded once again that those on the Other Side are not bound by dimensions of time and space as are we.

Jane and Joe have kindly read this book you hold in your hands. I consider it a remarkably gracious gesture, as to do so was to relive all the emotion around losing Bobby. I gently invited them to write their own words for inclusion but have not asked for an interview per se; it would simply be too painful for them.

# PART III

# Soul Planning and Your Life

# Chapter Nine

# A SPIRITUAL ROAD MAP

Perhaps like me, you're drawn to the mystical world. The realm of the unseen is captivating.

What I seek to present here is a simple primer of the concepts discussed in Bobby's Visit. Perhaps you're curious but unfamiliar with this type of content. Or maybe you'd like a sense of where I'm coming from. The journalist in me considered providing a much fuller, formally referenced literary review. However, that approach would have given the book a more academic feel. Instead, you will find a list of suggested readings, as well as a glossary for any unfamiliar terms.

In college, I began to read about near-death experiences (NDEs). We had been discussing cultural issues surrounding death as part of our coursework, and my curiosity piqued. We've all heard references to white light and tunnels. I was (and am) fascinated by what lies on the Other Side and in the angelic realm. I didn't doubt the existence of an afterlife, but like so many of us, I wanted to know what it looked like. Or, more accurately, to *remember* what it was like, since I believe that the Other Side is our true home base from which we come and go between lifetimes. I devoured *Many Lives, Many Masters* by Brian L. Weiss. This seminal book recounts the journey of a psychiatrist unearthing the past lives of one of his patients.

What follows is a basic road map to what I believe is a universal process. It is a combination of direct personal experience and extensive, joyful research. I suggest you read this from your spiritual center. Be guided by what resonates for you, and feel free to question.

My experience with Bobby's Visit included elements of an out-of-body-experience (OBE) and was spiritually transformative. At no point was I close to death.

**FURTHER READING:** ROBERT SCHWARTZ, *YOUR SOUL'S PLAN*; BRIAN L. WEISS, *MANY LIVES, MANY MASTERS*

## SOUL GROUPS

I believe each of us comprise a mind, body, and soul. The soul is our spark of the divine.

I further believe we travel in soul groups, encompassing many dozens or even hundreds of souls. We choose to be born into the same family or the same community—a connection that ensures we will cross paths. In this earthly realm, we play out different roles, *not for the suffering they entail, but for the spiritual growth they afford.* That's key. Growth in one soul helps the growth of the others, too. We learn from direct, firsthand experience but also from witnessing how other people live their lives and how they respond to challenges. We are finely and intricately connected. I find it helpful to remember that in our time here on earth, we are rather like actors in a play, fleshing out roles we have scripted and designed ourselves before we arrived. This can help lessen the sting from our most challenging or painful relationships.

Have you ever met a stranger and felt an immediate connection? Something resounds inwardly that can't be dismissed, though logic dictates you've had no time or opportunity to develop a bond. Chances are, they are part of your soul group. Our intuition acts as an internal compass. When I was a social worker, I met a new colleague who clicked. It happened that Jon and I were getting married just a few months later, and he was amused when I suggested we invite her and her partner to our wedding. Truth be told, I think she had the same reaction, though she graciously accepted. I simply knew, strongly, that she and her partner would become and remain close friends the rest of our lives. And decades later, she remains one of my most treasured confidantes.

A dear friend, an Orthodox Jew, told me about the idea of "Meeting at Sinai." The tradition teaches that all Jewish souls (departed, living, and future) were present with their *bashert* at Mount Sinai when the Ten Commandments were handed down to Moses. *Bashert* is often defined as "soul mate," but the term is infused with spiritual significance, beyond the romantic. The joyful challenge, once born, is to find one's *bashert*. I see parallels to soul planning, as this would entail *remembering* a divine plan, once born, to be lived out here on earth.

We'll be delving into soul planning in the next chapter. On that note, I highly recommend the books of Robert Schwartz. He distills his painstaking research into pre-birth planning in a compelling, conversational way. Especially fascinating are his transcripts of dialogue between souls and their guides.

**FURTHER READING:** MICHELLE AND EZIO DE ANGELIS, *POSTCARDS FROM THE OTHER SIDE;* MICHAEL NEWTON, *JOURNEY OF SOULS*

## PRE-DEATH

I recall being astonished in college when a social work professor shared that she and her siblings had not been allowed to sit at their mother's deathbed in the 1960s. The "white coats" (doctors) oversaw that sort of thing. Death seemed to be something that was clinically supervised, and the family was duly informed. Precious final moments were not recorded in hearts and memories but jotted as notes in a medical file.

Thankfully, Elisabeth Kübler-Ross and her pioneering work on death helped to chip away at these calcified attitudes and sparked changes that continue to ripple decades later. Her colleague Raymond Moody made the world sit up with *Life After Life*, his groundbreaking work on near-death experiences. The topic went from taboo to something openly discussed and debated in the general public as the phrase "near-death experience" entered popular culture. Today, some hospice staff encourage the family to verbally release their loved ones, giving them permission to move on.

There seems almost as many ways to depart this life as there are people. For some, death comes instantly; others experience a longer, drawn out goodbye.

For years, I had read and heard of deathbed visitations (also known as pre-death visions). This refers to the experience when people close to death sense the presence of loved ones who have passed over before them. They might see their long-deceased father, sitting in a chair by their hospital bed, smiling and patiently waiting to lovingly escort his child to the Other Side. Or perhaps a cherished grandmother shows up, who represents love and tranquility amid turmoil. These visits seem to occur with increasing frequency and clarity as the final moments to death approach. The message, whether "spoken" or not, is one of calm reassurance. Our loved ones from the spiritual world reach over to the earthly world to help us with our transition.

Propelled as they are by love, experiences like this emphasize the sheer interconnection between souls, and between physical and nonphysical planes. I appreciate that skeptics dismiss these experiences; they attribute them to oxygen depletion as death approaches.

**FURTHER READING:** TRUDY HARRIS, *GLIMPSES OF HEAVEN*; ELISABETH KÜBLER-ROSS, *ON DEATH AND DYING*; RAYMOND MOODY, *LIFE AFTER LIFE*; LISA SMARTT, *WORDS AT THE THRESHOLD*; HEIDI TELPNER, *ONE FOOT IN HEAVEN*

## SHARED DEATH EXPERIENCES

Imagine being at your mother's deathbed and seeing a mist rising from her chest or noticing dramatic changes in the light around you. Now picture the walls of the room appearing to bend during these final moments.

These are just some of the reports noted by Raymond Moody in his book on shared death experiences. In *Glimpses of Eternity*, he relates experiences by many people—doctors and nurses among them—who vividly witnessed and even participated in their loved one's journey. Some people reported accompanying their loved one part of the way into the light. Often, multiple family members were present to corroborate the experience.

Again, skeptics insist the brain releases a firestorm of chemical reactions as death approaches, which causes all manner of hallucinations. But, as Dr. Moody points out, this does not explain the attendant spouse or child, clearly not on the brink of death, who reports these experiences so vividly.

**FURTHER READING:** RAYMOND MOODY, *GLIMPSES OF ETERNITY*; MELVIN MORSE, *PARTING VISIONS*

## CROSSING OVER

Among the hundreds of cases of NDEs that I've read, people invariably related their "passing"—be it through a car crash, a seemingly routine operation, or a freak accident—with almost relaxed detachment. They described hovering above their body, some knowing instantly it belonged to themselves, others taking a while to make the connection.

In NDEs involving traumatic events, there are repeated accounts of the soul departing the physical body while there is still a heartbeat present. It seems we shrug off our physical forms as easily as we'd shrug off a heavy winter coat on a warm day.

**FURTHER READING:** EBEN ALEXANDER, *PROOF OF HEAVEN*; P. M. H. ATWATER, *BEYOND THE LIGHT*; MARY C. NEAL, *TO HEAVEN AND BACK*

# THE OTHER SIDE

I believe the Other Side is a place of complete, unbridled, and unselfish love, where no negativity exists in any form. I was raised, as perhaps you were, to think of clouds and harps when imagining Heaven. A taste of this sounds charming, but an eternity? Excruciating. I believe we happily take on an occupation on the Other Side, with none of the drudgery or obligation we might feel about our "work" here on earth. We don't "rest in peace." *We live out a joyful purpose.* I have pored over many accounts, for example, where people describe the happiness it gives them to greet children as they pass over, and to make the experience as welcoming and as nurturing as they can. We also enjoy leisure with loved ones and friends in our soul groups.

Perhaps, like me, you've wondered why so many people describe seeing a beautiful meadow when they cross over. This scene is often depicted in art, books, and movies. I imagine it's because a meadow seems familiar and peaceful. It's also a natural setting that takes many of us back to childhood—what child doesn't like to run around parks and other open spaces? Whatever the setting, the Other Side seems familiar. After all, a welcome home should feel familiar by its very nature, not disorienting. Young children who have survived NDEs describe being greeted by friendly beings with smiling faces and shown small, cuddly animals they're invited to pet. This smooths the way for an easier transition when it incorporates our personal or cultural frame of reference.

**FURTHER READING:** SYLVIA BROWNE, *LIFE ON THE OTHER SIDE*; BETTY J. EADIE, *EMBRACED BY THE LIGHT*

## REUNION WITH LOVED ONES

Once on the Other Side (however briefly), many people who have experienced NDEs describe a euphoria as they reunited with loved ones. It might be an aunt whom they adored, a sibling they lost early in life, or a best friend whose life was cut short. Others reported seeing beloved pets that gathered in a welcome chorus of chirping, meows and tail wagging. The first to greet us are those instantly recognizable from the life we just left. In addition, we are met by all our loved ones from past lives, too.

And it's here, this place of tranquility and love, that we remain until—and if—we choose to depart to live earthly lives, and to which we return.

## THE LIFE REVIEW

After the reunion comes an event called the life review. It is a chance for recently arrived souls to see their last lives on earth. Many NDE survivors describe scenes played back before them, often in panorama and taking various shapes. For some, the life review appears as a movie projected on a screen; for others, the pages of a book or even a hologram they could "step into" for a fuller immersion.

In reading various accounts, what stood out for me was that the same core elements appeared regardless of the person's culture or background. Whether someone had been black or white, rich or poor, educated or not—and, perhaps pivotally, religious or not—the life review was described in startlingly familiar ways.

I believe we relive the most significant events or moments in our lives from the perspective of our souls. However, what our *minds* consider significant may not align neatly with our soul's view. The soul is not concerned with outward accolades such as diplomas, trophies, or sports cars. The focus is on inner development. It's more about the moments when we shared unconditional love or extended support; when we held our tongue in anger to prevent hurting someone else. Likewise, we'll relive the time we took to welcome an anxious newcomer at school or work, and feel how it might have made all the difference to that person.

Small talk might not be so small after all, as it knits us in conversation and births connections. We also see the moments when we could have helped someone but simply didn't make the effort. We can more easily discern the ripple effects of our actions fanning out, whether good or bad.

Many of us have been raised to anticipate a harrowing Judgment Day when our sins are tallied and our fate handed down. If that is your belief, I respect it. But as others have articulated with far more eloquence, I believe it unfolds another way: We judge *ourselves*. This is the purpose of the life review. We examine our thoughts, words, and actions over our lifetime from a position of neutrality. And we do so without the self-defensiveness that springs from embarrassment. Ego is sidelined. We can watch the images unfold passively or from the perspective of the other people with whom we lived, worked, or met along the way.

Near-death experiences provide fresh insights on some of the life reviews, as in these examples:

> *In my last life, I treated work subordinates and custodial staff as lesser-than. I made assumptions about their character and didn't look beyond their position in the pecking order. At the same time, I had a kind side, supporting animal shelters and feeding stray dogs. I could channel some of that compassion into others.*
>
> —T. J., ATLANTA

> *I could see I'd become a needy person. I was a clingy child who grew into a clingy partner who needed lots of reassurance about being loved. This drained and alienated some people in my life. Other times, it attracted controlling types who liked to have someone to rescue. Next time, I might plan opportunities to develop more emotional independence.*
>
> —RAJNEESH, BANGALORE

Given that we do the judging, you might assume we're bound to breezily let ourselves off the hook for any questionable behavior. Not quite. In fact, those who have provided reports of their life reviews say it is our inclination to be harsher on ourselves as we register our full impact on others. Compassionate beings are there to pause the review when things get too painful. They infuse us with love and understanding, and we choose when to recommence the experience.

FURTHER READING: GEORGE ANDERSON AND ANDREW BARONE, *LESSONS FROM THE LIGHT*; DANNION BRINKLEY, *SAVED BY THE LIGHT*; MICHELLE AND EZIO DE ANGELIS, *POSTCARDS FROM THE OTHER SIDE*

## ANGELS AND SPIRIT GUIDES

As I saw in Bobby's soul-planning session, we are not alone when we review our lives. We do so in the company of our angels and spirit guides, the same ones who helped us plan that most recent life. I believe them to be different beings.

Angels are their own celestial species and, according to many religious texts, they were created before humans. Each major religion acknowledges these heavenly beings. We talk of deceased loved ones becoming our guardian angels, but as souls, we are different from angels. Members of the angelic realm can choose to incarnate briefly and are not bound by time and space. Hence, we hear stories of mysterious strangers arriving to assist in a fire or car accident, or in a moment of personal despair. Their arrival and departure are often brief and inexplicable, yet their impact is unquestioned by those whom they help.

Our spirit guides, by contrast, have lived many times in human form and for entire lifetimes. This equips them with a full spectrum of human experience, from jealousy to joy and recklessness to discipline. They have adopted widely disparate ethnicities, lived amid contrasting social classes, and practiced various faiths. This infuses them with insight and enables them to relate to a wide variety of circumstances and temptations. These guides, too, are free from constraints of time and space. Valuable spiritual insight must be attained before taking on the considerable responsibility but ultimate happiness of guiding other spirits.

I also believe our guides are from our same soul group, given the connection and trust that needs to exist between us as plans are designed on the Other Side and lived out on earth. I saw and felt this connection between Bobby and his guides. Imagine arriving at college for your first day, nervous about your workload in general or one subject in particular. Imagine then discovering your professor is an old family friend. She offers you extra help and guidance to see you through.

A spirit guide often chooses to stay on the Other Side while the soul they watch over heads to earth.

Significantly, many people also describe guidance from a prophet aligned with the religion in their most recent lifetime. For example, a Christian might be aware of Jesus, a Hindu might sense Lord Rama, or a Buddhist might be accompanied by Buddha. Notably, though, souls will often report *feeling* the presence of these deities, or seeing a light that surrounds them, emanates from them, or represents them, rather than being able to see their faces directly.

**FURTHER READING:** MARIE CHAPIAN, *ANGELS IN OUR LIVES*; JAMES VAN PRAAGH, *TALKING TO HEAVEN*; RICHARD WEBSTER, *SPIRIT GUIDES AND ANGEL GUARDIANS*

## PASSING THROUGH THE VEIL

The Veil of Forgetfulness, or simply the Veil, refers to the border between the physical and spiritual planes. When we plan our next life, we do so in the realm of the Other Side. We must arrive with a clean slate. If we're born with full knowledge of our divine gifts and access to every tool we'll ever need to cope here, then where is the learning curve? We may as well have stayed on the Other Side (which remains an option).

Instead, we arrive with spiritual amnesia. During our time here, some people will rediscover their spiritual core, others will flirt with the idea but not pursue it, and yet more will live their entire lives without being aware of their spiritual side at all.

In passing through the Veil, we transform from magnificent souls to mere mortals, bound by a heavy body and limited to just five senses. Quite a change. But at the same time, it's this exact experience that we crave, as the challenge of human limitations is not something we can access on the Other Side.

The process reminds me a little of movies or cartoons in which the characters shrink from their regular size, which enables them to have adventures in lands they couldn't otherwise access. As you'd imagine, their perspectives change drastically as, say, puppies appear to be the size of dinosaurs or a kitchen sink looms as large as the Grand Canyon.

## REBIRTH

It's not that we're "doomed" to repeat scenarios until we learn the lesson contained in them; I believe we're self-propelled to do so. We can see some measure of progress in our life reviews, but we're inspired to do more. We see it as an opportunity.

Returning is learning. That might sound worthy of a corny bumper sticker or meme, but in essence, I believe that is what drives us to keep coming back. We are thirsty to widen our experience and advance our soul's evolution.

For example, you might know (or be!) remarkably loving parents with a so-called problem child. You see the experience stretching them in new ways or driving them to distraction. It sparks growth at the individual soul level, but also for them as a couple and as a family unit.

It is *always* our choice to come here—and to choose not only the time and circumstances, but also the intensity of the lessons. We further decide if these challenges will arrive in rapid fire, seemingly piling on top of one another, or whether we'll sprinkle them through our soul plan at a more leisurely pace.

While we often choose our next life in response to our life review, I believe it's not always a knee-jerk reaction. Meaning, if we were wealthy in our last life, we might not automatically choose poverty the next time. We could plan to include it, or just as easily postpone it. This theme could be something we choose to encounter and embody over an arc of lifetimes—a "special series" that runs consecutively or between different themes. (More on life themes in an upcoming chapter.)

## KARMA

I'm interested in the way the term *karma* is widely referenced today. Like *guru*, it's a Sanskrit word with roots in Hinduism and Buddhism. According to the Oxford Dictionary, karma is defined as "the sum of a person's actions in this and previous states of existence, viewed as deciding their fate in future existences."

In popular usage, its meaning seems to be limited almost exclusively to "payback." We often cite karma when a person does or says something negative—perhaps something dishonest or unkind—and experiences a negative consequence. It's framed as outright punishment or a comeuppence at best. "They got what they deserved" is the verdict, whether delivered in a tone of righteousness or faint amusement.

I believe karma is broader than that, simply a balancing of experiences. If the Other Side represents only positives (with love at its core), then earth is our opportunity to experience the interplay of positives and negatives. Imagine someone has experienced only lifetimes of luxury and abundance. Might their soul want to experience financial hardship at some point (knowing it is temporary) for the chance to stretch and grow spiritually?

It can be disheartening to battle through life, waiting to catch a break. Meanwhile, we observe others who seemingly cheat on their taxes or spouses (or both) and walk away, scot-free. But we can never know the extent or intricacies of someone else's soul plan, nor how karma plays out in ways to which we remain oblivious.

Karma is not punishment. It's more about a balancing of energy and lessons between souls and among soul groups. If you had a past life in which you cared for a seriously ill spouse, the two of you might arrange to reverse the experience in a future life together, perhaps as spouses again, or as parent/child, or in a more formal arrangement. You would get to walk in each other's shoes, emerging with a much fuller sense of the caregiver-patient dynamic.

The Other Side is governed by divine and perfect order. Karma is one way to balance energy and experiences here on earth—without which I believe events would crumble into chaos.

**FURTHER READING:** EDGAR CAYCE'S ASSOCIATION FOR RESEARCH AND ENLIGHTENMENT, EDGARCAYCE.ORG; ANITA MOORJANI, *DYING TO BE ME*; GARY ZUKAV, *THE SEAT OF THE SOUL*

# Chapter Ten

# SOUL PLANNING

Soul planning, also known as pre-birth planning, refers to the process by which we choose our framework for this life on earth before being born. This occurs on the Other Side, or if you prefer, in Heaven. Before we arrive, we choose our parents, any siblings, and the time and country into which we're born.

If you have children, do you believe they came to you randomly or by design? Might they have easily been born to your friend, colleague, or the lady next door? Why this child, born into this family, at this particular time and place? These questions hint at the intricacy of a divine plan for each of us.

When you consider your own parents or any siblings, do you believe you might have chosen to be with them to play out certain roles as a means of spiritual growth? As family members, we often know how to "press each other's buttons." Might there be lessons in our patterns of communication?

Having selected the key elements of our lives in advance, we furnish details that will bring both opportunities and challenges. We craft the life lessons we'd like to experience, though once we've arrived we retain free will as to if and how we learn.

**FURTHER READING:** MICHAEL NEWTON, *JOURNEY OF SOULS*; PETER RICHELIEU, *A SOUL'S JOURNEY*; ROBERT SCHWARTZ, *YOUR SOUL'S GIFT*

## THE BENEFITS OF CONSIDERING SOUL PLANNING

The idea of soul planning is not for the faint of heart. It can raise difficult questions and lead us to wrestle with relationships or issues many of us would rather sweep under the carpet.

Yet I believe it also holds tremendous power to unlock the magnificence of our own souls, to view the universe—and our place in it—from a different and valuable perspective.

Have you ever felt weighed down by life's demands, as if you can't seem to catch a break?

We push through life on limited sleep. Our waking hours see us torn in different directions; everyone seems to have their hand out for something, be it our time, our energy, our attention. We crawl into bed at night, exhausted. Then we get up and do it again. Yes, there are moments of joy or a good belly laugh, but they can seem elusive and fleeting.

Other times, it can seem we're ambushed by random bad luck. At first, we might simply think this to ourselves. Then the idea takes a firmer hold, and we speak it out loud, lamenting our misfortune to others. If we don't harness that negative self-talk, it can become a label we adopt for ourselves and eventually the way we are viewed by others.

Let's turn that around. Karma is not ensnaring us. We are not cursed, nor is our family. Instead, what if we're traveling a path that is self-designed and self-chosen? One that is adopted willingly?

When we explore the possibility that we design and choose our own life challenges, it changes our perspective. We move from a point of victimhood, where bad things happen to us, to a place where we can cope. We change from reacting to our experiences to being proactive in having chosen them—again, not for the suffering they entail, but the growth they afford.

When we even *consider* that we design our life lessons, it stops us from feeling blindsided, as if the world is against us. It infuses purpose and opportunity into our days and our trials. We are no longer leaves blowing around in the wind at random; there is a divine plan for each of us. A plan of our own design.

## WHY WE COME HERE

There are two major differences between earth and the Other Side. The first, as I mentioned earlier, is that on the Other Side, negativity does not exist: love permeates everything and everyone. From what I saw of Bobby's Visit, we exist there as our highest selves, the genuinely best version of who we are. There is no judgment, suspicion, rivalry, or other earthly emotions or behaviors. The second difference is that the Other Side is a place of theory, while earth is a place of practice. Here, then, is where we get to put the theory into practice.

Imagine the finest medical school: all theory, but with not a single ill person to examine, diagnose, or wheel into surgery. Its doctors could be superbly trained in all manner of medical science, but their education—and their role as healers—would be severely lacking without living, breathing patients to treat.

Alternatively, picture earth as a school playground: all manner of personalities and relationships abound. We experience close friendship, looser social connections, and bullies. As the children play games, some follow the rules, while others cheat without a second thought. Cliques form, and alliances are forged, some lasting, some fleeting. It is where some students practice kindness, as others learn patience or develop self-esteem. Conflict rears its head and is solved in a variety of healthy and unhealthy ways.

Whichever imagery or metaphor you prefer, the crux of soul planning is to plot challenges from which we learn. No one signs up for a perfect, error-free path. To do so would defeat the central

*plot challenges from which we learn*

reason we come here at all. Mistakes are not viewed as setbacks on the Other Side; it's how we *respond* to them that matters. Whether we admit our mistakes and take responsibility, or blame others, our responses serve as the basis from which we can grow, better know ourselves, and develop spiritually.

That said, our time here is not driven exclusively by challenges. We absolutely plan moments of joy, and relationships and friendships that are sources of love, amusement, and laughter. Our plans are a patchwork quilt of human emotion and experience.

We plan positive and negative lessons. For example, when we experience the joy of unconditional love—something we don't need to earn but receive simply because we exist—we learn how to show it to others. We win the trust of a child, and realize that this is a gift and a lesson in itself. Similarly, when we forge a bond with an animal, especially one that one has been mistreated, both sides benefit.

When we encounter pain, we grow from it. We find ourselves coping with situations we'd never have imagined, and a new reality sets in. We discover a stronger, more resilient core at our center.

And always, someone is watching: our children, a friend, a neighbor. They learn, too, from our journey.

## WHY WE RETURN MULTIPLE TIMES

Any lesson worth learning takes more than a single attempt to master. This is true for anything from archery and boat building to stand-up comedy. Why would our soul's development be any different?

Extensive spiritual growth takes more than one lifetime. When we consider lessons such as patience, unconditional love, or emotional independence, a series of lives seems necessary. Add to that, a lifespan of seventy or eighty years is a blink of an eye compared to eternity.

Mistakes allow us to choose responses

At our core, our souls yearn to taste it all. We draw from a river of experience each time we stretch beyond our comfort zone to grow and evolve our souls. We relish a steady infusion of variety, as well as fresh challenges and growth arcs, so we choose contrasting cultures and countries in which to live.

Any discussion of rebirth would be incomplete without acknowledging the life's work of Dr. Ian Stevenson from the University of Virginia. He documented thousands of cases of reincarnation (and not a single Cleopatra or Leonardo da Vinci among them!). He garnered attention for his case studies of children exhibiting xenoglossia, also known as xenoglossy (from *xeno* meaning foreign and *glossia* meaning language). These preschoolers could converse fluently in languages, including obscure dialects, to which they had never been exposed. The cases studies even included children who spoke so-called "dead" languages from ancient civilizations. This phenomenon suggests that these languages were carried over from previous incarnations and somehow left a cellular imprint in the children's current lives.

All this coming and going naturally invites questions: How many lifetimes do we live? And how do we know when the last one will be? I believe the actual number varies for each of us, according to our free will. Many spiritual teachers mention hundreds of lives for one person. That might sound alarming or even tedious, but it is always our own choice whether to come here. I believe our cycle ends when our souls have learned and extended every facet of service to another, experienced every type and intensity of relationship, and encompassed the entire spectrum of human emotion.

In *Your Soul's Plan*, Robert Schwartz writes:

> *We do not and indeed cannot complete our cycle of physical lifetimes until we have left our accumulated wisdom on the Earth plane.*

I love that idea—both its essence and its reciprocity. It brings to mind revered spiritual teachers who greet death with grace, content in both what they have experienced and the knowledge they have imparted to others. It has symmetry: as we close this chapter, we open the door for another by sharing our insights.

**FURTHER READING:** CAROL BOWMAN, *CHILDREN'S PAST LIVES*; TRUTZ HARDO, *CHILDREN WHO HAVE LIVED BEFORE*; ROY STEMMAN, *REINCARNATION: TRUE STORIES OF PAST LIVES*; IAN STEVENSON, *TWENTY CASES SUGGESTIVE OF REINCARNATION*

## KEY DECISIONS TO BE MADE

In cultures worldwide, the family unit is a core way in which we organize and socialize. Thus, in our planning sessions, we carefully choose our parents and any siblings, along with any religious affiliation. We choose our looks and any idiosyncrasies, such as a charming gullibility, a propensity to sweat profusely, or a tendency to be a martyr. We choose our ethnicity, our sexual orientation, and in turn, the potential for discrimination to varying extents.

Our spirit guides navigate us through a maze of options regarding the who, what, and where of our upcoming life. The key building blocks are significant: we choose the country we are born to, whether a rural or urban area, the era in time, and, as noted above, our family. These alone, I imagine, can take many planning sessions.

We also decide whether we're likely to marry, and if so, we choose our spouses. As we plan this detailed framework, we still retain our free will. For example, I believe I planned to meet my husband, Jon, in this lifetime. But it remained our choice to be passing ships, to enjoy a summer romance, or to kindle something that would last our entire lives.

# PUBLISHING OUR SOUL PLANS
# IN THE AKASHIC RECORDS

As we've seen, we invest tremendous time and energy into our soul plans. When the fine-tuning is complete, a record (also known as a chart) is made of our future plans. It's a joyful declaration of our intent for our upcoming lives. We pledge these charts not with dread or out of obligation, but with excitement, eager to tackle our upcoming lessons. (While on the Other Side, we can also access and review the plans of all our previous lives.)

Many spiritual authors have referenced the Akashic Records, also known as The Book of Life in religious texts. It is said that once we complete the designs of our chart or plan for this life, it is recorded here for eternity. The renowned spiritualist and clairvoyant Edgar Cayce often said that when he read for clients, he was accessing their soul plans from the Akashic Records.

**FURTHER READING**: EDGAR CAYCE'S ASSOCIATION FOR RESEARCH AND ENLIGHTENMENT, EDGARCAYCE.ORG; DEBBRA LUPIEN, *AKASHA UNLEASHED,* DR. LINDA HOWE, CENTER FOR AKASHIC STUDIES, LINDAHOWE.COM

# THE ROLE OF FREE WILL AND INTENT

I believe everyone on the Other Side has the gift of free will. Angels, spirit guides, and souls like us all have the option to exercise choices as to their words and actions.

Even as we plan our upcoming lives, we retain this gift to use at our discretion. Finally, and crucially, we retain free will once we're born.

It's at this point, when we arrive on earth, that our soul plans and our lives can diverge like a fork in the road. We design charts with the best of intentions . . . and then life intervenes, with all its demands and stressors. On arrival here, we are separated temporarily from our higher selves. Naturally, we think and behave as the human beings we are.

While I believe our soul plans feature intricate detail, it doesn't mean our lives become robotic. Far from "going through the motions," we infuse considerable nuance in our designs, weaving in more soul contracts and varied exit points.

Others believe we have the option to choose loose frameworks, specifying only the crucial elements such as our country, time, and family. This type of plan might be chosen by souls who want more fluidity, and it might include fewer exit points. I am open to this possibility, as so many options are made available to us on the Other Side.

You might believe life is a string of random happenings; I believe we each have a divine plan of our choosing and with God's loving support. The intent we exercise in life is powerful and brimming with its own vibration. Consider the simple act of giving. We might give something valuable freely and joyfully, and we might give something invaluable begrudgingly. The intent around any given action or thought carries its own vibration. The focus or purpose we use to direct our efforts, from anger management to patience, helps set the course; even if we miss the mark, the universe acknowledges our good-faith attempts (and it also sees through token gestures). Our intent speaks to how we direct our energy and activity, beyond simply wanting or desiring something. It contains more deliberation, more willfulness toward a desired outcome.

Once the main framework is decided, we look inward to the challenges we might wish to work on and learn from in this next life. We choose what to focus on for the next stage of our soul's evolution. And that's where our life themes come in.

*Chapter Eleven*

# LIFE THEMES

Themes are the overarching lessons we choose for our next life. They are challenges we seek to work on and hope to eventually conquer. I believe themes reflect not only our specific goals—a part of our character we'd like to further hone and polish—but the wider mission our soul is seeking to work on in this upcoming lifetime. That said, they do not dominate our every waking moment. Rather, they can form a quiet but significant backdrop to our lives.

It's part of human nature to fall into patterns of behavior and communication. A woman I used to work with would bemoan, "I always choose the wrong men. My mother calls me a professional doormat." A neighbor, who has been divorced three times, openly admits each spouse took him to the cleaners. When we reflect on our own lives, any recurring challenges can hold clues to our life themes. I think back to my social work days, and I wonder if those young clients who were adopted or grew up in the foster care system were bravely grappling with ideas of abandonment or rejection. I can only hope they eventually found love, security, and self-acceptance. When we take a moment to imagine someone else's circumstances, we can more easily find compassion.

The families we're born into form a template as to how we communicate, which is why they're involved in how our themes play out. They shape how we see ourselves, the wider world, and our place in it. They influence how we express ourselves verbally, emotionally, or physically. From our families, we might learn to resolve conflict through tantrums, time out, calm negotiation, or physical violence. We learn about personal space and privacy, and through that, what forms healthy or unhealthy boundaries. In turn, we craft a blueprint for how we will be as parents, adopting some elements of our childhood while rejecting others.

Common themes might include developing qualities such as self-esteem, patience, and willpower amid this family unit and beyond. Themes might also encompass issues such as time management, leadership, or cultivating a sense of personal responsibility. Others might elect to work on empathy or maintaining a sense of identity amid a family of strong, overpowering personalities.

I believe as we plan our themes, our spiritual guides offer nonjudgment and patient listening. Drawing on the benefit of their own experiences on earth, they might prod us to plan a gentler pace. They might remind us, for example, "You've scheduled a significant health diagnosis around the same time your company downsizes and your job is at risk." Or suggest, "The loss of your mother is only months before legal issues arise with your neighbors—would you like to give yourself time to catch your breath?" While they embrace our creativity, they also feel a sense of protection toward us.

Living our lives means living out our themes, whether consciously or unconsciously. Let's look a little closer at some widespread themes and dispel a few myths along the way.

**FURTHER READING:** SYLVIA BROWNE, *LIFE ON THE OTHER SIDE*; ROBERT SCHWARTZ, *YOUR SOUL'S GIFT*

## SELF-ESTEEM

We might embrace lessons around self-esteem to better discover and retain our worth as a person. In this case, it wouldn't help much to surround ourselves with relentless cheerleaders who praise our every move. We'd get much more opportunity to learn if we placed ourselves among some critical family members. As they—wittingly or unwittingly—label us in disparaging ways, we have a choice to buy into that or to forge a different identity.

A mother who is hypercritical of her child might provide a crucial lesson in developing inner strength against a soundtrack of condemnation or sarcasm. A chauvinistic father could likewise be playing a part to help his child develop assertiveness or a clearer sense of self. Being raised by such a personality might lead a young woman to rebel and see herself beyond traditional gender roles. We not only engage parents to take on scripts for us, but siblings, grandparents, and friends.

I once knew a man in California who was severely embarrassed by his father's occupation. He used to half joke that in his culture, there were few acceptable professions: doctor, lawyer, dentist. Before I met his parents, this man fabricated an elaborate story to prevent me from discovering what his dad did for a living. He said his father was an ophthalmic surgeon but had to give up his life's work due to his own failing eyesight and that this was a source of intense emotional pain. He now wore thick "Coke bottle" glasses. In fact, his father was a salesman, and was a gentle, kind, and generous man. I said a silent prayer that Mr. P. would never discover his son's shame. I was disgusted by the son; I judged him. Today, I regret my judgment, and I wonder if he is working through his own themes of self-worth.

## RESILIENCE

Imagine you've chosen to focus this lifetime on a theme of resilience. You want to attain the strength to keep going amid setbacks, real or imagined. If you plan a life entirely of smooth sailing, you'll be denying yourself the rich learning opportunities to emerge stronger and to tap your inner strength. You might miss the chance to ever know yourself as a survivor.

Or you might elect to be the family "black sheep" to develop inner strength and a sense of identity. You might plan to move to a community with different beliefs or values, which you might respect but not adopt, or which you might openly fight against. Either way, you'll likely be on the "outs" socially, politically, or otherwise. On a more practical note, you might decide to experience a temporary marriage, which affects your financial security as it dissolves. You might also choose to be an ethnic minority, to feel directly how it is to be marginalized.

## PATIENCE

I'll put my hand up for this one.

Perhaps more than at any time before, patience seems an increasingly rare commodity today. We live in a culture of instant gratification, where the mere expectation to wait for something or someone seems almost quaint. The ability to wait our turn, tolerate delays, or explain ourselves repeatedly further strains our reserves of elusive serenity.

Any mother or father knows the creative ways a small child can devise to delay bedtime. They'll plead for one more story, an extra hug, a glass of water, or a bathroom visit. This nightly ritual can be exasperating for an already tired parent and would test anyone's patience.

Likewise, if you have a loved one with dementia or work in aged care, you know the broken record of questions and answers can wear you down. Each inquiry is posed with fresh curiosity, though it was asked and answered only moments before.

Patience is a quality demanded in our fast-paced world, from our personal relationships to dealing with customer service departments. It makes sense, then, that many of us would choose to work on a theme that develops a healthier tolerance of delays or a better capacity for self-restraint in the face of disagreement. We value that which is rare, and patience fits the bill.

## OVERCOMING ADVERSITY

We find inspiration and role models in those who triumph over hardship, be it humble beginnings or surmounting a physical impairment. Culturally, we delight in rags-to-riches stories, such as a struggling single parent winning the jackpot. It dovetails with a popular worldview of struggle before reward. This makes a theme of overcoming adversity more relatable.

A life of daily struggle isn't hard to spot. We've all experienced and observed how adversity can take many forms. Some misfortunes arrive as major one-time events that spark long-term effects. These might be a car accident, a severe and progressive medical diagnosis, or a job loss that erodes into homelessness.

Adversity needn't be extreme to breed despair: a more moderate but constant struggle to pay bills can wear away at us and prove just as debilitating as a major life tragedy. We see people worn down by life, enduring a struggle that depletes their spirit and hopes for a better future. Others endure toxic relationships with family members, which seem to form a destructive backdrop to their world. They bring physical, mental, emotional, and financial burdens.

Poverty can refer to a more general sense of want beyond financial struggle. It can encompass a poverty consciousness, where someone adopts a mindset of "not enough": not enough time (provoking constant stress or resentment), not enough love (sparking jealousy), or not enough opportunities (sowing the seeds of fierce competitiveness). When viewed through these prisms, a theme of poverty yields plenty of insight for souls who choose it.

## OVERCOMING PRIVILEGE

Humor me for a moment.

Picture someone whom you think has it all—perhaps a person you know or a public figure. They appear to have won the lottery of life, never knowing heartache or financial strain or career disappointment. We may think we know them intimately; they might even be in our family. But *everyone* struggles with something, regardless of whether we're privy to it.

When these "victors" do share their troubles, they're likely to be mocked or have their setbacks or heartache dismissed. People both shut them down and shut them off.

Let's broaden this out. Some children of celebrities seemingly have everything, but they lack purpose. They make headlines with their drug abuse or other reckless behavior, drifting without a compass. As their family connections open doors, they lack a sense of having earned respect or accolades. They also tend to be resented, especially if they are deemed to be parading their lifestyles on social media.

Others are born into a family of academic or athletic overachievers, and feel they have no hope of matching up. They often strike out in an entirely different direction to escape expectations and inevitable comparisons that come with the family name.

What we might call a "cushy" life could be full of silent challenges—either things we cannot discern on the surface or aspects they fight to keep in the shadows. As a child protection worker, I saw the effects of horrific abuse play out in beautiful homes with idyllic settings. You would have thought the people in them lived storybook lives.

Perhaps you know someone who always seems to land on their feet—and maybe, sometimes, you feel a twinge of resentment or envy for their seeming good luck. To an outward observer, it appears that events always fall in their favor. But we don't know the lessons they have designed.

FURTHER READING: NEALE DONALD WALSCH, *CONVERSATIONS WITH GOD, BOOK ONE*

## LEARNING HEALTHY BOUNDARIES

I once had a social work client who was crumbling under the pressure of family obligations. In any given week, there were multiple get-togethers to celebrate occasions from the significant to the ho-hum. Barring arrest, a flesh-eating virus, or being trapped under a bus, the expectation was to be there. And nothing was off-limits to family: siblings and cousins knew each other's salaries, mortgages, and medical issues. Amid this oversharing, Gina craved solitude and privacy.

In time, she gradually came to see her family as less "close" and more enmeshed. She gained a lot of ground—against much resistance—in reframing her role in all this. Month after month, she deflected guilt trips, emotional bartering, and outright fury. She drew her line in the sand and set healthier parameters. By embracing a theme of boundaries, Gina reclaimed her time, her emotional independence, and her autonomy.

## SERVICE TO OTHERS

Through soul contracts, each of us acts in service to others for our mutual learning. Whether we are linked through family, a workplace setting, or a fleeting connection, our themes play out.

Many souls go beyond this to choose themes more solidly framed around a life of service. They might pursue traditional helping professions, such as teaching or nursing. A service theme might involve devotion to a cause, such as child advocacy, or something seemingly tangential, such as raising puppies to be service dogs. We may never know or even meet the people who benefit from this service, but the ripple effects nonetheless fan out.

Others perform a more subtle service by being effective listeners. Consider how many people feel invisible or unheard in our society. They are undervalued or marginalized in some way. The gift of active listening—genuinely engaging someone, unrushed and face-to-face—shows that we value the other person. We might disagree vehemently, but there is value in the exchange.

## WHAT IS YOUR LIFE THEME?

I asked people via social media to look at the key relationships and patterns in their lives for the clues they might hold to their own life themes.

> *A head on a pillow: That's my key memory of my mother all through elementary school. She suffered a stroke in her thirties when my sister and I were small. Even today, when I think back, I only ever picture her in bed with a gaudy bedspread pulled up to her chin.*
>
> *I grew up watching my father care for her, and we all had to pitch in. I resented it until I saw how tired he was when he sank into his chair at night. I ditched my college plans to give Dad a break. I planned to go later, but I never did. She's still alive, and I campaign hard for euthanasia rights. No way this is happening to me. Yeah, I'd guess my themes are caregiver and activist.*
>
> —RABIA, ISTANBUL

*Look at key relationships to find life themes*

*OK, this is hard to admit, because I'm in my forties. But I've never been able to finish anything. My parents say when I was a kid, they had to force me to stick to a sport or hobby for more than two weeks. Ballet, crafts, swimming, you name it—I reveled in it, then tired of it. Pretty normal, I think, for that age. Only it kept going. In college, I changed my major three times. Never graduated.*

*I used to see a therapist. She said deep down I don't think I'm worthy. Don't know if I buy that. But I'd have to guess my theme involves commitment and discipline.*

—JANA, SAN FRANCISCO

*Communication, for sure. They said I was just naturally shy. That's OK as a kid. As a manager? Not so much. Growing up, three older brothers talked over me. At work, I struggled to get my ideas out in meetings or to assert myself. On a personal front, my ex-wife was fun but loud. Her big personality let me retreat into the background. I'm on my own now, and in the last twelve months, I feel like I'm making inroads in speaking up. Small steps, sure, but they're there.*

—NIRMAL, HOUSTON

*This sentence cost me thousands of dollars (in therapy) to write: I have always identified myself primarily as my body.*

*As a child, I was molested. My body's misuse defined me as a victim. Then I gained weight to protect myself, and every day, through puffing and panting, my physicality made itself known. At age twenty-seven, I lost more than a hundred pounds and even flirted with bodybuilding. Only now am I learning to embrace my mind and spirit.*

—M. K., OXFORD

*I asked my partner what he thinks my theme would be. He said impulsiveness. I look back, and I have a history of not thinking things through.*

*I once signed a lease on an art studio because I'd taken one short course in sculpture. Suddenly that was all I wanted to do. I used to move in with boyfriends within weeks, but in my defense, it's not like I was looking to get married. Actually, I almost agreed to tie the knot in Vegas once in a drive-through chapel, until my friend slapped some sense into me.*

*But it's not all bad, or even that serious. I'm the friend who will rock up to your door on a miserable gray day and convince you to go to a belly-dancing festival. I'm creative and always have good ideas on stuff to do. Just keep me away from anything that requires a signature.*

—KATYA, NEW YORK CITY

*Maria la pacifista (Maria the pacifist). That was my nickname. School yard squabbles, high school fights, tension at work, family drama: you name it, I was in the middle, trying to be a peacemaker. One day, I realized I was so uncomfortable with any sort of tension, I was shutting down healthy debate. I try to resist the impulse to agree at all costs—because it ends up costing me.*

—M. J. P., HOUSTON

*I'm a natural loner, and I fight it daily. My career in research limits contact with others. I'm not socially awkward; I just like my own company. But if I don't change, my solitude will no longer be a choice.*

—A. J. JR., SEATTLE

# *Chapter Twelve*

## SOUL CONTRACTS

Having chosen our themes from a wide and varied menu of potential human experiences, we then make agreements with other souls to help these situations manifest.

Imagine that in a past incarnation, I was reckless in my approach to life and acted a lot on impulse. I made hasty decisions that sparked regret or made plans without a firm foundation. In planning my next life, I might choose to make a soul contract with a future parent who is planning to become physically impaired in his forties, when I'm still a small child. Watching him tackle physical limitations daily, I'll have a chance to develop a healthy respect for life and a realization of how it might change in an instant. This could be a singular or even simple observation, but the effect on me might be profound.

Or perhaps in early soul-planning sessions, Soul A meets Soul B, who is planning to explore a temporary but intense mental health issue such as postpartum depression. Soul A might make a contract to appear as Soul B's spouse or indeed her baby, who might either bond well or experience early emotional detachment from his mother. Contracts such as these always give me pause for the magnificence of the souls who plan them.

Contracts can offer a helpful framework and ensure that souls arrive with overlapping lives, with themes that better correspond to create a richer learning field. And in the process of aiding each other to work through our checklists, we, too, grow spiritually.

## THE DYNAMICS OF A SOUL CONTRACT

Soul contracts play out in myriad ways, with a vast array of themes, variables, and personalities. In general, most agreements are made for the mutual benefit and learning of the souls involved. In that sense, the dynamic is essentially one of give and take.

However, I believe some plans are designed so that one soul can choose to play out a role in the background, allowing the other soul to take center stage this time around. Further, there are particularly selfless souls—sometimes called "lightworkers" in broader spiritual literature—who postpone their goals entirely for a lifetime in order that others may shine. These are the unsung heroes in our families and wider communities. They work quietly and inconspicuously, neither seeking nor attaining recognition.

## THE ACTOR FACTOR

*All the world's a stage, and all the men and women merely players; They have their exits and their entrances, and one man in his time plays many parts . . .*
—WILLIAM SHAKESPEARE, *As You Like It*

Let's give Shakespeare's words a twist, courtesy of the Other Side. When we design our soul plans, we're essentially writing a screenplay for our upcoming life. Our script has a setting, an era, and a cast of both headliners and more peripheral characters.

And crucially, it has a storyline. To flesh out our plot, we assign parts to others (soul contracts) as a vehicle through which our story plays out. In other words, the actors have roles with purpose. Even with free will, they initially agree to play characters within a set rationale and story arc rather than speaking and acting at random. After all, we might indulge in some "improv," but it happens within a wider framework.

Among the twists and turns, we include moments of joy, growth, jarring revelations, and peaceful routine: the theater of life, as it were.

When relationships are in bloom, it's easy to imagine having chosen each other to share this lifetime. When our roles are combative or damaging, it's hard to see their purpose. Harder still to even consider the possibility that we would choose these dynamics.

As we live out these scripts, remembering "the actor factor" can help take the sting out of a given role, whether it's, say, a partner who is hypercritical or a "golden child" sibling whom you might have resented while growing up. Viewing a role as one part in a play creates distance and a dash of impartiality. What is happening might be viewed as less "personal." This offers a prism to better understand our interplay. It helps to contemplate that the people most cruel or dismissive of us are playing a role we have scripted for them.

The play reaches its climax, and we take a final bow. With that, we peel off our theatrical masks and see each other for the joyful, loving souls we are. We will commend each other for a job well done, and any feelings we felt on earth will dissolve along with the temporary characters who portrayed them.

Let's expand that from one life to a series of lives or screenplays as our souls evolve. When we view and select from the variety of lives open to us, both past and future incarnations, it's as though we're veteran actors who change costumes in rapid fire. We seamlessly and masterfully adopt different accents, ages, or even postures and manners of walking. In the lives he showed me, Bobby was always male, but I believe we choose our gender during our soul-planning sessions. Nor does it appear that gender was crucial to the life plan he was designing.

If the people who cause us the most pain are simply adopting a role we requested of them, do we learn the strength to walk away? Do we crumple, or learn assertion and demand better treatment?

## THE VOLUNTEER

In my twenties, I volunteered at a consumer organization. One day, another helper shared something intimate out of the blue.

She told me she had found herself pregnant in her late teens, too afraid to tell her strict parents. Her boyfriend was physically abusive and controlling, but she knew no different and (much worse) didn't think she deserved better. She scrimped together her money and took a bus to another town to have a termination. There, she endured the entire ordeal without anyone to hold her hand. Alone and scared, shivering in her hospital gown, she whispered to her baby, "I'm so sorry, but I'm not ready for you right now. Please come back to me." Many years later, she became pregnant again with a baby girl. Her relationship with the father was once again violent, but because of her infant daughter, this time the woman found the strength to leave. She told me that she is certain that her child today was the spirit she was not ready to welcome the first time.

Her experience shows me the tremendous compassion and nonjudgment between souls, and that her child understood the circumstances into which she would arrive the first time were not ideal. This soul was willing to return when her mother had matured. And it was the mother's love for her daughter that gave her the final push to take a stand and to break a pattern of domestic violence. (Of course, women who struggle unsuccessfully to escape abusive relationships also desperately love their children.) Where once there was fear, she found courage.

When I recall this, I think of the soul contracts we make with each other. While the daughter came back quickly, she also had the option to return in say, five or ten incarnations down the road.

We have so many nuances and options from which to select when planning an upcoming life.

**FURTHER READING:** CAROL BOWMAN, *RETURN FROM HEAVEN*; CAROLINE MYSS, *SACRED CONTRACTS*; IAN STEVENSON, *CHILDREN WHO REMEMBER PAST LIVES*

## OUT OF THE MOUTHS OF BABES . . .

I sought experiences from parents whose children had ever mentioned a different family member, home, or circumstance.

*We have twin boys, and they're total live wires. I've learned to tune out their tussles over toys, whose turn it is, and who is better at something, so I'm not sure what made me listen closer this time.*

*Kyle was winning at something (or so he thought) and Ben was adamant, "You always do this! I'm never going to be born with you again!" I got goosebumps, and Ben was on a roll. "You promised! You promised in the sky you'd let me win more. It's not fair."*

*I put them in quiet corners and spent a few minutes with each. As I consoled Ben, he said, "I love you, Mommy. You're a good mommy. I was a good daddy when we were poor, and I made you wooden toys."*

*Gulp.*

—PAULA, MELBOURNE

*It was Mother's Day, and our children had made a tea party as only a three-, five-, and seven-year-old can. As we were sipping our pretend tea and eating our pretend cookies, our middle child, Mica, gave me a cute card she'd made. As I was oohing and aahing over it, I noticed a second card. "That's for Granny," she said. "Before, I was a boy in her tummy. But I wanted to keep playing with Jesus and the girl (?), so he let me. I said I'd come to you next time, so we can all be together."*

*My mother had lost a boy at seven months. None of my children could have known this.*

—GABRIELLA, SYDNEY

*I was babysitting my niece, and I got her drawing with my four-year-old. They had a great time until the tears erupted. Can't remember what for, but I'll never forget the next part. I told them to say they're sorry. Then I insisted they say one nice thing to each other. I waited. Nadia said, "You let me go first with the doll house." Her cousin said, "You're kind to animals." Then her face lit up as if remembering something. "Like my horse when we were soldiers in the war! He was scared because the knife cut him (a bayonet?), and you made him go quiet and happy. He was licking your hand like Snoops (our dog), then he closed his eyes."*

—FREYA, GLASGOW

*Chapter Thirteen*

# EXIT POINTS

The Other Side is a place of divine and perfect order. Given how much effort we invest in planning our lives and the circumstances in which we enter them, it seems reasonable that we would also consider the ways in which we exit our lives. This, too, is a source of learning, both for us and those around us. I believe souls invest tremendous time and effort in designing their exit points. They plan a setting in which not only they learn a tremendous amount, but so does their immediate family and wider community.

Exit points are essentially off-ramps. These points are planted along a lifetime so that the soul can decide if it has learned enough or simply all it *wants* to learn in this incarnation. Many authors of spirituality have referenced three to five exit points as being a popular number, but there appears to be no hard and fast rules as to their quantity or timing. They are not methodically spaced and can be placed together in quick succession. Many souls, Bobby among them, choose to include one exit point before they are physically born; I believe this might help explain the common occurrence of miscarriage.

Before we go further, I'd like to share a wonderful example of how accepting our exit points (whether or not we label them as such) can foster healthy attitudes toward life and death. You might recall an essay in the *New York Times'* Modern Love column that went viral, in which a dying woman invited readers to consider marrying her husband. Amy Krouse Rosenthal eloquently described their relationship and showcased her partner's many qualities. What really captured me was that she understood her journey this time around was drawing to a close but his was continuing, and she wanted for him to find someone new with whom to share life's joys and trials. Amy grasped the impermanence of it all, and far from begrudging him a new companion, she all but took out a billboard. I loved that essay, and through it, I loved her.

Now, a look at some common exit points.

**FURTHER READING:** SYLVIA BROWNE, *BLESSINGS FROM THE OTHER SIDE*; AMY KROUSE ROSENTHAL, *"YOU MAY WANT TO MARRY MY HUSBAND,"* MODERN LOVE, *NEW YORK TIMES*, MARCH 3, 2017; ROBERT SCHWARTZ, *YOUR SOUL'S PLAN*

## CAR ACCIDENTS

Given the sheer number of roads and cars on the planet—not to mention the emergence of road rage—it should come as no surprise that car accidents are a common exit point.

For more than a decade, I kept a crumpled, faded clipping of a news story. Through each house move or spring cleaning, I couldn't bring myself to discard it. I found it compelling. It tells of two brothers who died in separate car accidents, only minutes apart. I think of their young lives snuffed out in near-identical circumstances on different sides of town. I try to imagine the impact on their parents and how they came to terms with their loss.

As sad and shocking as the story is, there seems an overarching order to it all. To my mind, it can't be dismissed as coincidence. There is far more at play.

When I share stories such as this, others often reciprocate. When I first began in journalism, a veteran cameraman told me that a colleague was dispatched to film the scene of a traffic fatality, only to discover the deceased was his own child. More recently, a friend recalled a neighborhood police chase. The young car thief needed medical attention after slamming the vehicle into a tree. And who was the ambulance driver assigned to the call? The teenager's father. Anecdotal? Yes. They're also true.

## TERMINAL ILLNESS

"Cancer can be a blessing." I was taken aback when I first heard this. But some patients have told me, despite the months or years of pain, rotating hospital admissions, and financial strain, that it is better to have time to prepare for their death than to pass suddenly. It allows them space to get their affairs in order, to heal rifts, and to leave nothing unsaid to their loved ones.

A terminal illness is especially poignant when diagnosed early in life. It goes against every natural order for a parent to bury their child. I can only imagine the depth of their pain and the feeling of brokenness inside. I'm not sure anyone really "gets over" the loss of a child, though perhaps, at best, one comes to terms with it.

Each illness has an individual arc to how it unfolds. There are so many variables. What condition will it be? How severe? Will the person survive or not survive? Will they direct their time, energy, and resources to exploring experimental trials? What if they participate in the trials, still pass away, but the research helps save future lives?

In our society, we attach significance to the way patients face their final days. We applaud those who fight on and vow never to give up. I believe doing so helps assuage our own fears around death. If the patient is encouraged to deny the possibility of death, we can push our own dread aside. What about someone who bravely accepts a terminal diagnosis, whether on day one or six months in? At what stage does acceptance come, if at all?

Sometimes a "fighting spirit" is simply *fighting our spirit*, resisting what our souls have planned.

Consider someone you know who you has undergone a major life event, be it cancer, a serious accident, or a near-death experience. To my mind, no one emerges unchanged. Whether or not they discuss it, we often observe a shift in priorities. For some, a close brush with death unleashes fresh urgency. They're suddenly planning trips they've long postponed. Others are inspired to leave an unfulfilling job or relationship to follow their hearts. Or you may have noticed a subtler effect, such as an overall slowing down to savor life's small joys. The reactions are as individual as the person concerned, but they are there.

## COMAS

Like sleep, a coma is an altered state, whether or not it is medically induced. I believe it is chosen by some souls as part of their plan and agreed upon by the family members who are navigating them through that journey. It affords time for inward examination, so souls can decide whether to return to their earthly life. They can throw up their hands and surrender to events as they unfold, or they might discern some finely tuned options. I believe people in comas can hear what we say in their presence. Some NDE survivors say they decided to return to their bodies after hearing their loved ones pleading for them to come back. While in this state, souls are in contact with their angels and guides to help decide the next step.

## SUICIDE

I've not lost a loved one to suicide, so I cannot speak to the pain this sears into the heart of a grieving parent, sibling, or friend. All I can offer is this: I am not directly aware of suicide being deliberately chosen as a possible exit point from the Other Side. I do recognize that despair can take on a truly dark and heavy presence in our lives.

I'm not seeking to glorify suicide or soften its impact in any way. However, I believe souls who are driven to take their own lives are shown tremendous compassion once they arrive Home. I want to emphasize this because so many people spend years grappling with their loved one's transition and worry that they are being punished. Far from being left to drift aimlessly, I believe these souls are infused with extra care and love as soon as they arrive—even before a reunion with their loved ones. I believe souls return complete, beautifully whole, when they arrive back on the Other Side. They bear no marks such as scars or burns which might reflect how they ended their earthly lives. Crucially, I believe the soul departs the body before physical death.

Our angelic guides recognize the emotional state surrounding those final moments. With loving patience, they gently guide the soul back to a state of spiritual equilibrium. The Other Side exists in balance and in harmony.

In coming lives, with the benefit of insight from the life review, the soul has an opportunity to revisit the issues they left unresolved by ending their life. This is not a punishment, more a chance to learn a postponed lesson.

A suicide is likely to have an impact on any soul contracts made with others. Those people, in turn, will have their own reactions to contend with, in both the immediate aftermath and the longer term.

## "FREAK ACCIDENTS"

A so-called freak accident appears to defy odds or explanation. It is heartbreaking enough when a fatality is deemed accidental; the "freak" nature of a bizarre incident suggests something even less anticipated and more unforeseen. Unless the victim was willfully taking on a risk, we can struggle to see any rhyme or reason for such an event unfolding.

As humans, we might view a mishap as so unlikely and news-worthy that it falls into this category, such as a person being sucked out of a plane window midflight, contracting a rare trop-ical disease, or being struck by a stray bullet. From the point of soul planning, these occurrences are simply creative options by which a soul can depart this life. They form a tapestry alongside more common (but no less devastating) occurrences such as fatal allergic reactions, heart disease, or stroke.

## SOULS WHO PASS IN INFANCY

My sister Marian lived a matter of hours.

Both the pregnancy and her birth were precarious, and tragi-cally she was gone by sunset. It is difficult to fathom today, but my mother was not permitted to hold her newborn; the doctors deemed it too traumatic. She has only the soap used to wash her baby girl. I have heard the story retold many times, and yet even now, I feel the tears prick.

I believe that Marian is part of my soul group, that she agreed to be born into our family to play her brief but pivotal role. Her short life left an indelible mark on all who knew her or knew of her.

I'm often asked, What life lesson could anyone possibly learn from mere hours on earth? Marian learned the joy of uncon-ditional love in utero and on her arrival. We tend to think of lessons in a negative sense. But we gain understanding and fresh insight from all sorts of circumstances, from the jubilant to the exasperating.

In turn, Marian gifted my family an opportunity to learn. She inspires me to reflect on the scale of our connections; she did not become part of my family at random. I believe her soul plan was chosen to coordinate carefully with those of my parents. I imagine that amid their shock and grief, my mother and father were pre-sented a choice. Would they become mired in sorrow and retreat from the world? Or would they summon all their inner strength to keep going for their other children? I don't mean they were "taught a lesson" in a punitive way. I mean that one cannot endure heartache and loss on that scale without emerging stronger and more spiritually evolved.

Marian is just one example of a soul arriving in service to others. While every death triggers pain and sorrow, the loss of an infant or child sears far deeper. But perhaps, many months or years distant, the passing and purpose of these little ones can eventually be seen through a different prism: as a catalyst that sparks tremendous spiritual growth in others. This potential for growth is not limited to their parents and siblings, who will, of course, feel their absence most severely. Depending on the specific cause of death, a soul's premature departure could also help others in the wider public by engendering new safety regulations, fresh medical research, or criminal justice reform.

*Chapter Fourteen*

# MISCONCEPTIONS ABOUT
# SOUL PLANNING

So far, we've looked at the general process, based on Bobby's Visit and other sources, whereby we design our soul plans before we arrive back here on earth. We've explored life themes that we might choose to work on and exit points that we might select to depart this life. I respect, as mentioned early in the book, that some of these topics might be painful for you to consider, especially if you are dealing with profound loss or hardship.

It's vital to address some key misconceptions about elements of soul planning. Let's begin with the question asked most often.

**Is being born with a disability, or acquiring one during life, a sign of punishment?**

*Absolutely not.*

Having a disability, whether physical or psychological, is not a punishment. In fact, I believe it to be a powerful sign of an advanced soul. This was central to what I witnessed in Bobby's soul-planning session. To be willing to take on these challenges—or even the possibility of these challenges—is not for the faint-hearted.

**Does poverty indicate that someone is paying for bad karma in a past life?**

Poverty is not a punishment, nor is wealth a reward. It might seem tempting or easy to draw these conclusions. We're simply working through different roles. Just as an actor might play a prince or a pauper onstage, so, too, do we play different characters in our various incarnations. Our spirit guides do not value money (nor do we, as souls, while planning our next life). However, they witness in the earthly realm that money motivates many people, for better or worse, in how they behave and the life choices they make. They recognize the main elements in which we work and live.

**It's easy for people in the developed world to proclaim that suffering is a learning opportunity. Their lives are not an endless cycle of misery and toil.**

Yes, it is easy to make these claims while we eat from full plates, enjoy hot showers, or slip into warm beds. Allow me to return to a simple but potent tenet: from the point of eternity, a lifetime of seven or eight decades seems short indeed. Our souls recognize that as real as our suffering will be while on earth, it is also equally true that we will be back on the Other Side soon.

**What about abusive relationships? Are you saying we chose these? That we deserve them?**

This point is vital to clarify.

Categorically, no one—no one—deserves to be abused, in any form. When relationships are marked by trauma, it becomes harder to contemplate why anyone would be involved in such a life plan—be it as a key player or more peripherally.

There is a major difference between one soul choosing a theme and another soul deserving any outcome from it.

Our family members or potential spouses might decide on particularly difficult themes to tackle. These might include overcoming anger management, which could involve challenges around physical, emotional, and verbal self-discipline. As they attempt, successfully or unsuccessfully, to overcome this issue, others around them might suffer. But adult individuals, too, have a choice and learning opportunity—for example, to develop assertion (versus aggression) or to draw healthy boundaries. Again, this does not mean anyone deserves to suffer abuse.

Another soul might choose an addiction such as alcohol or substance abuse, which in turn could have a lasting impact on those around them. While other souls might be aware of this plan and the potential for addiction, they, too, have a chance to grow in how they react. Will they adopt a "tough love" approach or become an enabler? Of course, there is a full spectrum of reactions in between.

Crucially, themes such as these are designed to be confronted, not indulged. It's never an excuse for someone to throw up their arms and claim, "See? I chose this. I can't help it." The point is to accomplish work on this theme and to grow spiritually in the process.

## Why would anyone choose to have horrific things happen to themselves or their loved ones?

Here's the thing: We design our soul plans with the noblest of intentions, from the peaceful realm of the Other Side. Then we arrive and enter the "real world."

We forget our soul plans (our charts) because the point is to start with a clean slate. I don't believe anyone gleefully plans to experience or enact horrific events. I do think that our incredibly wise souls know the propensity for humans to fall short of the mark in the goals we set. Also, we don't "choose," as such, the risk of anything happening to our children or other loved ones. But we might bravely agree to support a soul who will arrive as our child and who is choosing some dangerous exit points. Traumatic outcomes can result from us veering off course, either willfully or despite our best efforts. We all retain free will and can abandon our plans once we're here.

**What about the perpetrators of horrific acts? Were their crimes part of their soul plan?**

Others have written about crimes being planned, including heinous behavior such as rape. At first, I recoiled at these suggestions; today, I maintain an open mind. I do believe some souls choose to grapple with exceedingly difficult plans. Once here, they are separated from their higher selves and have passed through the Veil of Forgetfulness. They also have free will to veer entirely off their paths, to behave in a way that would cause trauma to others.

I don't believe you need to fully embrace the concept of soul planning in its entirety to gain insight. You will know what resonates and what doesn't. For example, if you have lost a loved one to violent crime, it is understandable that you may not be willing to entertain the possibility that they chose this manner of death. I respect that. Potential perpetrators, unfortunately, have free will as to how they live their lives. They have made a series of decisions, or one seemingly random decision, that led to a violent act. I do not seek to tell you how to feel.

All I can suggest is that you look to the outcome of that loved one's death for possible clues. Beyond the immediate aftermath, what ripple effects fanned out in your life and in the lives of those around you? Did your family unit grow stronger? Did someone turn to (or back to) their faith? Was anybody spurred into activism, demanding tougher laws or penalties? Did someone else who was previously adrift snap into focus as to what they wanted out of life? The aftereffect might be much subtler, not seeming at all related to the manner of a loved one's exit point. Granted, these things can be learned without such a painful trigger, but we feel invincible at the time we design our plans.

**If only the good die young, what does that say about those who live to 100?**

A long life does not mean someone has extra lessons to learn or is slow to learn. They have simply chosen to forgo earlier exit points in favor of one in advanced old age. In turn, their extended presence in the lives of their loved ones sparks its own opportunities for spiritual development.

# PART IV

## The Aftermath

*Chapter Fifteen*

# MY THEMES
# (AND MAYBE YOURS, TOO)

As I reflected more and more on Bobby's Visit, I naturally explored my own potential themes. I offer two examples here, and they each happen to involve a parent. I hope they encourage you to explore your own themes.

### FINDING MY VOICE

When I was in middle school, family friends from India stayed with us.

The "uncle" (not actually a relative, and in this case, an undeserving honorific) made me uneasy, but I couldn't articulate why. One afternoon, he called me into his room to help him find something. My knees went to jelly, and I stayed glued to the doorway, mumbling that he should check under the bed. I was nervous to do this; in our culture, it's not taken lightly to refuse an elder, and a houseguest at that. At this time, my immediate family had no idea as to the risk he posed.

The secret would not emerge for more than a decade. In my twenties, I visited the man's wife in India. She shared that he had abused their granddaughter from age seven to age eighteen, stopping only when she became pregnant. Yes. You read that correctly.

Over time, I tried repeatedly to report this man in his hometown, and I alerted other women in his family. (In India, intergenerational living is the norm.) In short, his wealth insulated him from repercussions. The language barrier didn't help; I spoke neither Hindi nor the regional dialect. This meant I couldn't get past the domestic staff who usually answered the phone.

I thwarted his efforts to vacation in Australia by filing preemptive reports with the Federal Police. I later learned he was not only vacationing in the US, but staying with a family who had young children. I contacted authorities, who made their own assessment and removed him within hours.

What unfolded in the aftermath was exceedingly painful. In short, my mother supported her friend (the wife) and forgave the perpetrator. She further disowned me for bringing the issue to light; this is a very common reaction to an age-old problem. The man's family, meanwhile, made multiple death threats to both Jon and me, and vowed copious other ways to ruin us.

Amid it all, a voice whispered, *You chose this.*

Again it came, in moments I was actively reflecting on the incident, or else immersed in something else entirely. *You chose this.*

And I knew it to be true. I knew it in my head, heart, and gut. I understood there would be ugliness and threats in taking the action I did. However, inaction was unthinkable.

But my sense of knowing went beyond that. In the bleakness of the year that followed, I felt strongly that in a past life, I had not spoken up. I had witnessed something, or at least knew of something, but had stayed silent. I had lacked the courage to find my voice. Rather than being punished, I was now being given a chance to repeat the lesson with the aim of growth. (It also explains to me why I was propelled to a first career in child protection.)

The experience was grueling, but I know that I grew spiritually from it. Portals opened in my heart and mind as to why this might have happened. Jon and I grew even closer for what we navigated together. Despite disbelief and disappointment, I could eventually step back and acknowledge that my mother had lived decades of good works. This incident did not define her. However, it did define our relationship. I believe we planned a soul contract for me to experience rejection from a key person in my life. I retained free will to acquiesce or to take a stand.

I came to view this ordeal as connected to an experience I shared with you earlier, in which I was shown I had planned a potential life lesson when my car brakes failed. In that scenario, I could have been responsible for my sister's teenage death, and in turn, felt the rejection of my mother. As that event did not unfold (thankfully), I experienced her rejection in a different setting. Either way, you see, the chance to evolve spiritually was going to present itself.

The relationship with my mother never healed. Contemplating a soul contract, with its goals and outcomes, made it easier for me to live with. I know that once we both cross over to the Other Side, we will see more clearly the roles we played and the insights they yielded.

I would take the same action tomorrow.

Speaking up. Handling rejection.

Whether in a cutthroat career or from within my own family, these themes have intermittently woven in and out of my life. To be clear, my life is not all about rejection! Not by a long run. I absolutely know acceptance in terms of a loving husband, sister, in-laws, wonderful friends, and a measure of career success. And by experiencing love and acceptance from my youngest days, I was able to extend that to others.

Reviewing my themes helped me see parallels.

- Why was I drawn to volunteer in a hospice in India? These people, the poorest of the poor, felt their own rejection in society, albeit on a far more severe scale.
- Why volunteer at the leprosy hospital? I always felt I was drawn there because leprosy is as much a social disease as a physical disease. The patients there, too, felt rejection, outcast by their communities. While knowing my efforts were a drop in the ocean, I was still compelled to try to ease their suffering.
- Finally, was I propelled to become a child protection advocate because of some faint blueprint in a past life, when I did not speak up about abuse? Was I seeking a chance to do better with a course correction this time around?

I also wonder about another possible reason I chose not to have children in this lifetime: given the rejection by my mother, was some part of me concerned I might repeat the pattern with a child of my own? Having seen how Bobby's spirit guides encouraged him to consider various outcomes, I cannot dismiss this possibility.

### FINDING MEANING AT THE END OF LIFE

It is no coincidence that as I sit down to write this, my father's days are drawing to a close. Both parents showered me and my siblings with love, stability, and generous hearts. They gave us our sense of morals and principles, together with an education and our faith—all the tools we needed to carve out lives of our own.

Dad is in his nineties and has dementia. While it is heartbreaking to witness, I can only imagine what it is to endure. He has windows of lucidity, and for that, his family and friends are grateful. He doesn't know our names, nor does he need to; we simply want him to feel safe, loved, and well fed.

Some years ago, living in a different country and aware that his mental capacity was dwindling, I began to talk directly to my father's soul. I believe anyone can do this. I accept his mind and body are deteriorating, but his soul is vibrant. It has infinite clarity, ready to communicate at any time. I am certain Dad receives these messages. You might have heard of Padre Pio, a priest (later a saint) who was known to send his angels to others. We can do the same. Why not? They are, after all, messengers.

Watching an elderly parent become frail is a near-universal experience. Dad is tired, and he's done with this life. He retains just enough mental faculties to know how much he has lost. He cries out to God and begs to be taken Home. We are not privy to my father's soul plan and what lessons he might have designed. But whatever they are, surely, he has addressed them by now?

Then I wonder, Is he staying for *us*?

He may well have learned all the lessons he crafted, but in hanging on, perhaps he is giving us the opportunity to grow spiritually. The way we or any children react to a dying parent can be as varied and individual as the way we grieve (and the goodbye often starts long before physical death). On any given day, a child or caregiver might feel inspired, defeated, patient, a touch resentful, or quietly nostalgic.

On days when we are mentally and physically drained, we may think that God is refusing to call Dad Home and is making him suffer, but I try to consider another perspective. What if God is honoring my father's soul plan and the timing of his exit, lovingly holding steady while Dad himself is wavering?

I'm certainly not the only caregiver for my father; there are six other children living in town who also play their part. Dad has always been a quietly dignified man. I have witnessed lessons in grace as I have seen him deteriorate physically and finally accept the help of others. He has given me the chance to observe humility and humanity. And whereas the rejection from my mother was swift and final, Dad has gifted me a far more gradual release. Even on the harrowing days, I'm grateful for the chance to leave nothing unsaid. It is bittersweet that moments later, he will forget the words we share quietly between our prayers and his slumber, but his soul is faithfully recording them all.

*Chapter Sixteen*

# THE IMPACT OF BOBBY'S VISIT TODAY

I view life differently since Bobby's Visit. How can I not? I'll read a news article on a married couple of sixty years who died minutes apart and it prompts me to reflect on the spiritual synchronicity of a shared exit point.

I reflect more on the belief that we each hold in us a spark of divinity. We gain so much when we look inward. As I mentioned early on, no doctor has ever biopsied a soul. No scientist has ever studied one under a microscope. But it's there. And while we have the choice to embrace or ignore our spiritual side, it offers us so much.

No one is left unchanged by a spiritual experience, whether it involves a brush with death or a glimpse into another dimension. Some people experience depression, as they ache to return to that heavenly realm. For some, the overwhelming takeaway is renewed appreciation for life itself. They are less likely to crave the approval of others, and more willing to claim the life that is theirs. They are driven to begin anew, reorganize their priorities, or make amends.

Allow me to share some ways in which my own views have changed since meeting Bobby.

## SPIRITUAL IMPACT

### My Approach to Death . . .

I think about death every day, if only for a moment. I find it helps sort out what really matters. In fact, contemplating my mortality made it easier to take off my journalist hat to write this book. If my account of Bobby's Visit helps ease a sense of loss for others, even for just a few people, that will mean more to me at the end of my life than having read one more bulletin or filed one more story.

I'm also reminded about "the gift of a good death." When I worked at the hospice in India, the nuns would talk of a good death as a final loving act. To make someone comfortable, to afford them dignity, and to honor their passing was a gift to both involved.

I no longer fear death. I don't believe for a moment we disappear into some black void. I do sometimes wonder *how* my death will come—will it be with a gunshot to the back of my head, as I saw at age seven? Will it be at the end of a long life, in my sleep? Or something different altogether?

I reflect more on how a fear of death drives many of the actions and choices we see unfolding around us. An addiction to cosmetic surgery, an affair with a younger person, even the proverbial mid-life purchase of a sports car—these are all ways we help stave off our fears of aging. A friend believes that ageism is rooted in a fear of death.

We have many euphemisms for death. We say our loved ones have passed on, transitioned, gone Home, gone to God, changed energy, or simply expired (a favorite in India). These expressions are more palatable than saying someone died. I don't mind *death*—it's a word we endow with too much power, like refusing to say the C word. What is cancer but a cluster of diseased cells? I don't say that to trivialize its impact for a moment, only that I'm not sure avoiding certain words achieves anything. Then again, if it helps someone navigate a difficult time, who am I to say?

Personally, I like to think that we graduate. We leave Home (the Other Side) the first time as preschoolers, and return (after a cycle of lives here) as college graduates, eager to share the knowledge we've attained.

My views on the timing of death have also changed. In light of soul planning and our free will to plan our exit points, you could say that we all die right on time. Do I run around saying this at funerals? Hardly. But I hear from so many people that they are wracked with guilt at not having made it in time to say goodbye to their loved one, and I wish for their sake that they could see that everyone goes when the time is right for them. For *them*.

If you were to pass away tomorrow, your loved ones would feel differently, to say the least. Amid the emotions that consume us in grief, anger at being abandoned is only natural. I can't imagine, for example, being left alone with children to raise. Or being a child and enduring the loss of my mother or father so early in life.

People wrestle with anguish because they fear their loved one died alone. They punish themselves for not making the flight, or taking a wrong turn, or not picking up the phone when the call came that, to their mind, would have made the difference. They further blame themselves, and it becomes a toxin that seeps into all areas of their lives.

Add to this an unresolved argument or long-standing rift, and people can torture themselves for months and years. But here's the thing: they are attaching earthly, human emotions, such as anger or resentment, to a nonearthly dimension. Such negative, dense emotions simply are not present on the Other Side.

## . . . and My Approach to Life

I have a deeper appreciation for how unique we each are. It might be cliché, but the truth is, there is no one else quite like you, or me, or any of us in this world. We are each a glorious mess of imperfection, and there is beauty in embracing that—both our flaws and our gifts.

When I was younger, I traded off parts of myself in order to please someone else or to gain the approval of others (whether wittingly or unwittingly). Today, people are welcome to take me or leave me as I am. While continuing to be a work in progress, I'm no longer willing to trade off my essence. I *take responsibility* for who I am, but I do not *apologize* for who I am. I offer that with quiet assurance, not aggression. I know I will continue to make mistakes and to grow from them. I choose my battles and reserve my energy for speaking my truth. If that sounds like a crusade, it's not. If anything, I indulge more in silliness and laughter. People before pursuits.

And while I am more discerning as to whom I spend time with, I am also more inclined to make room for a wild card—be it a person, a belief system, or a pastime that will encourage me to broaden my horizons. If I don't, life will become a stifling echo chamber of like-minded opinions and worldviews.

While Bobby's Visit was life altering, it doesn't mean I have all the answers. But it did give me more clarity on what matters and what doesn't in my life. That said, I don't think you need to experience something on that scale to gain this insight!

## Contemplating the Life Review

I think about my life review in some form each day, whether fleetingly or in meditation. What have I thought, done, or said today that I would cringe to have to relive? It might be momentary, or I might contemplate it extensively with introspection. Usually, though, it's a few minutes in the shower (so that it becomes as routine as brushing my teeth).

glorious imperfection

daily life review

With Bobby, I saw depictions of past lives. I watched them passively (though with fascination). When I next have a life review, it will be much more immersive. I believe I will see all the times my thoughts, words, or actions hurt others (eek!) and also the times I brought joy and eased heartache. I will experience the impact on the other person. I keep a sign on my desk: *life review*. It reminds ← me to hold my tongue in anger because I don't want to have to relive that moment.

## Realizing We Are Never Alone

Bobby's Visit reinforced to me that we are never alone in life. Sometimes, we can feel helpless, or emotionally isolated, or simply misunderstood; these are all different forms of separation from others.

In our moments of darkness or joy, our angels and guides remain by our side. They are a deep source of strength, comfort, and love. And while beautiful, flowing prayers abound, I think we can talk to these compassionate beings as we would an old friend. Whether we need a steady drip of support to see us through a challenge, or something more akin to a gushing fire hose to dampen our fears, we can summon that help effortlessly.

Mother Teresa said that loneliness was as much a hunger as an aching, empty stomach. It's something we can all help ease, with a kind word or a friendly wave.

## Accepting Our Impermanence

You might say life is the ultimate limited-time offer. (This time around, anyway.)

When we accept—truly accept—that we, our lives, and every- ← thing in it are temporary, it is freeing. It is genuinely liberating.

It's part of human nature that we form bonds with other people; a shared history enriches those connections. We further form bonds with things: a family heirloom (no matter how modest), our first car, or that box of baseball cards in the attic we can't bring ourselves to give away. But we all know the simple truth is that no one and nothing lasts forever. We can choose to cling to something ever more tightly and fruitlessly, or to acknowledge its impermanence and take time to really enjoy it in the present. Buddhists say it is our attachment to impermanent things that sparks suffering.

It is also said that we grieve to the extent that we love. I don't think this means that we should love any less to spare ourselves future heartache, but perhaps instead to consider that no one we continue to love is ever truly separated from us. The entire core of Bobby's message was that *he did not die.* His energy changed form. He remained close by, feeling his family's love and sending them his.

I was reminded of this recently. My phone broke, full of photos and videos of my elderly father. I treasure them, and in that moment I feared I had lost these visual connections to him. But as upsetting as it was initially, I later realized I'd not reacted with half the loss I would normally have experienced. I could lose all photos of my father, and as sad as that would be, I know I will see him again.

I've learned to pause and relish the joyful moments, and to plow through the challenges, knowing there is an end. Setbacks won't last forever, and I'm prompted to seek the purpose in them.

I worry less. I more often ask, "What's the worst that can happen?"

### Things We Carry Over from One Life to the Next

I believe we arrive back on the Other Side whole and perfectly complete. I believe my sister Marian arrived in Heaven with none of the physical impediments she experienced in her brief time here.

I also believe that we carry over all manner of insights and lessons from each lifetime; learning is the reason we come to earth at all. This includes a recollection of *how* we died, even if we did not suffer at the moment of death itself. Residual imprints from a past life can help explain fears and phobias carried from one life to the next. To be clear, we don't suffer from these fears when we return Home. We are in harmony internally and with everything and everyone around us.

If I rolled up my sleeves, I could show you half a dozen pairs of dots, close together. They resemble snake bites, and I am open to the possibility that they represent a past death by reptiles. Celtic Druids would routinely check a newborn for birthmarks, considering them a way to discern how the person died in their previous life. (I once had a python strung around my neck for a feature story. I agreed in the hope it might cure me of my fear of snakes, but on one precondition: Just tell me it's well fed.)

Once we master a particular lesson, we move forward with the benefit of insight. We take them with us. For example, someone who was spent several lifetimes wrestling with a controlling nature will take their newfound insights with them. That lesson is complete.

On a brighter note, we also carry over insights from lessons learned. We needn't keep repeating the same mistake or dynamic. Similarly, talents honed over lifetimes may arrive with us; these are the child prodigies.

When I read of a child virtuoso—think Mozart composing at age five or Picasso turning heads with mature works as a teen— it makes sense to me that these gifts and skills were developed before arriving here. Each of these prodigies possessed more talent than anyone can muster—or master—in a single lifetime. Our prior lives and lessons leave both a spiritual and cellular imprint.

## Valuing Our Intuition

I heed my intuition more readily. I believe our intuition is our souls whispering, willing to guide us if only we choose to let them. Our angels and guides can also reach us though this "inner knowing." We can harness help far beyond our earthly five senses for guidance.

## The Benefits of Meditation

And how do I sharpen my intuition? I meditate now. I enjoy guided imagery. It creates a peaceful oasis. When I retreat within, I tap both my individual essence and the interconnections we have with each other. I am reminded that to help others, I help myself, and that to hurt others is to hurt myself.

I recently read that meditation was being taught in some inner-city schools in the US, where students endured challenging home lives. I was elated that these children were introduced to this outlet. Both their grades and their behavior improved dramatically.

## PERSONAL IMPACT

### Emotional Responsibility

Despite the progress I've made, I still cave into daily frustrations. Yet when I indulge in a flash of anger or impatience, something whispers beneath it: I know the reaction I'm having at that moment is a *chosen* response. I am *choosing* to become frustrated, and likewise I can opt to dispel that feeling.

### Self-Acceptance

I saw and heard Bobby choose his ethnicity and his looks for his upcoming life. It's something I reflect on often.

Our bodies are our physical coats this time around. During our soul-planning sessions, we give careful thought to our outer appearance, from our basic build, to minor details like that funny tip at the end of our nose or the shape of our ears, to physical traits with more serious implications.

If we truly took our choices to heart, we would more easily channel self-acceptance. Many people—especially women—dedicate significant time, money, and other resources to altering their

*Every reaction is a chosen response*

appearance. How much kinder might we be to our bodies if we accepted the idea that we chose them.

This idea of self-acceptance came home to me in a simple but lasting way: I'm now far less anxious about having my photograph taken. A small thing, granted, but you see, I have dodged photos for years. And I have taken a "selfie" exactly once—after I hurt my eye and snapped a picture to show the doctor. Bobby's Visit showed me that being too embarrassed to step into frame was effectively erasing me from mementos of my marriage and my friendships. Who cares if my hair is wild enough to scare animals and small children? If someone wants to capture a moment, that's more important.

## The Role of Intent

The intent we show in life is powerful and brimming with its own vibration. We're not machines, going through the motions of our daily routines robotically. The focus or purpose we use to direct our efforts, from charity work to patience, helps sets the course of our lives. Even if we miss the mark, the universe still acknowledges our good-faith efforts. Intent speaks to how we focus our energy and activity. It's beyond simply wanting or desiring something. It contains more deliberation, more willfulness toward a desired outcome.

## SOCIAL IMPACT

### Friendship

I was intrigued to see the "support crew" that showed up in Bobby's soul-planning session.

There was Mike, who was part of the extended family. He offered companionship, understanding, and a rich vein of support in Bobby's journey ahead. Far beyond cheerleading, this connection, I believe, would have offered real insight to Bobby. As Mike was to arrive first, he could offer the experience of someone older.

Then there was Krishna, Jane's friend. She was willing to find time—to make time—to support Jane through an extremely difficult part of her life.

Equally, I believe our friendships here on earth are often planned to serve a divine purpose, after which they may endure, morph into a different sort of connection, or dissolve. Of course, there may be many variables as to how this plays out. I recall a saying: "Friendships last only as long as there is a mutual need." At first glance, this view may seem a bit harsh, as if to imply, "Let's use each other, then move on." But, as I'm sure you have experienced too, the connections are far more nuanced than that.

We might be brought together by a shared age or stage in life, milestones, or passions. In time, one friend outgrows the other or simply grows in a different direction. I think about all the anguish that goes into lost or frayed connections (glance at any advice column), when really we could just wish each other well at the end of a soul contract. Of course, there are compassionate ways to release someone, but even with the best intentions, it doesn't always work out that way.

I find myself returning to an old adage: "Friends come into our lives for a reason, a season, or a lifetime." Though many of us experience a core group of long-term friends, this saying can make it easier to recognize the value of more fleeting but pivotal connections, and to release them joyfully.

As I have written this book and shared its journey with friends, I have been very grateful for the support and feedback they have offered. I'm touched by those who have read the manuscript even though it is really not their cup of tea. I have felt one or two begin to pull away a little, as they perceive me in a different way now than in the past. They struggle to reconcile the "old Alicia" with what they read in these pages. In my twenties, this would have devastated me. Today, as sad as that feels, I am thankful for the years and milestones we've shared. Moving forward, I can see a time when we might release each other with good wishes (spoken or unspoken), our bond gently ebbing away. Whenever something like this happens, we each create emotional and spiritual space to welcome connections with people who are perhaps more aligned to who we are today. This in no way diminishes the value others have brought to our lives in the past.

## Time Alone

And as much as I appreciate time with friends, Bobby's Visit inspired me to enjoy a little more time alone for balance. In my first book, I wrote about FOMO, the Fear of Missing Out. At the time, it referenced a feeling of people driven to keep up with their friends and colleagues via social media. A few years on, I'm delighted to see more written about JOMO, the Joy of Missing Out. It seems more of us are inspired to enjoy our own company, and to take a break from external distractions. This is restful for us in mind, body, and soul.

## Marriage

When the souls known as Jane and Joe stepped into the circle as Bobby's parents, they did not appear to be married as we would understand it. They chose to come together to play the roles of husband and wife for Bobby and their other children. They did seem to come from the same soul group, though, and displayed a recognition and relaxed familiarity that suggested prior incarnations together.

I emerged from Bobby's Visit with the strong feeling that while marriage is often chosen as part of a soul plan, it is not necessarily designed to last until death-do-us-part for every coupling. I don't intend to sound cavalier about that. I mean only that a union is planned as a vehicle through which different lessons unfold: not only for the pair concerned, but for any offspring and extended family too. Have you ever known an in-law who was heavily invested in a child's marriage or overly concerned about how grandchildren should be raised? Lessons play out between and among all sorts of relatives and friends. Once the divine plan has unfolded, the soul contract has been honored.

Those of us who are, or have been, in a long-term relationship—whether legally married or not—can recall days when marriage is, by twist and turn, a safe haven, a battleground, a summer school, and a sanctuary to catch our breath. It can variously be a question mark, an exclamation point, and a period.

Equally, the aftermath of any separation or divorce may also serve to enrich our spiritual development. We can be quick to equate failure of a marriage with personal failure, yet it can take tremendous strength to recognize a relationship is no longer honoring the people in it. It can be harder still to make the break amid cultural, religious, or familial backlash. Imagine all the ways people on earth punish themselves—or judge others—by considering divorce as a failure. Sometimes I wonder if we confuse success with longevity. Meanwhile, those on the Other Side view separation or divorce with impartiality as the learning ground it is. Consider someone who must learn to trust again after betrayal or rebuild self-esteem after an emotionally controlling relationship. Therein lies growth: painful, to be sure, but also a vehicle for evolving one's soul through new experiences.

There is always a variety of coping mechanisms in the event of a marriage breakdown. People understandably carry anger and bitterness and might seek refuge, for example, in addictions. In time, they might build resilience, emerging with a firmer identity and sense of self-worth. Others choose to not confront the reasons behind a breakdown and repeat these patterns in future relationships. The outcome contains vital clues to the soul growth planned.

I have witnessed friends, loved ones, and colleagues berate themselves for a marriage that ends in divorce. They struggle under the weight of family pressure, compounded by social and religious expectations. Their grief eclipses their memory of the good years, when they grew together, laughed together, and learned together. I sincerely believe that the option for marriage is considered during our soul-planning sessions, and depending on the lessons contained within, the relationship is designed to endure or to reach an impasse.

## Interactions with Others

I take people less at face value. We can never know what silent battles they are waging inside.

For example, I recently went to renew my driver's license and found the customer service representative exasperating; he was so slow, it was like he was running through wet cement. I wanted to say, "I could do your job in a coma. Underwater. And half ravaged by sharks." I did not. (Some days are better than others.)

I also try to remember the vastness of people's souls and to not be focused on their outward shells. For example, when I see or meet nonverbal children, I think about how they are profoundly expressive on the Other Side. They are wearing a temporary costume this time around. Perhaps they are gifted singers or eloquent orators, currently putting aside that skill set they have already mastered while they craft others. It helps me to be more aware of each person's magnificence.

I feel that significant life lessons can be found masquerading as everyday moments in life.

## Judgment

I'm a bit slower to judge (OK, I can still roll my eyes with the best of them). Sometimes, though, I find trying to imagine their themes can help to deal with difficult people. I don't suggest you share your thoughts unless invited! Even then, proceed with equal parts caution and kindness.

When we view a circumstance with judgment, we inflict suffering on others. As humans, we can be vicious about subjecting each other—and ourselves—to judgment of our actions, words, or life choices. This can calcify into hatred or self-hatred and destroy relationships. The saying "We become what we judge" carries more impact these days. It refers not to a punishment, but to a balancing of experiences. If I spend a lifetime looking down on a particular group of people, I will see this in my next life review. I will likely want to register the impact of my assumptions and attitudes, and to experience being on the receiving end. I will weigh this decision from a point of neutrality.

### The Toxicity of Pity
No one deserves to be pitied.

If I see someone dealing with a challenge—be it physical, financial, mental, or emotional—I try to take a moment to tune into whether I'm feeling compassion or pity. Pity evokes sympathy, but it is also imbued with judgment of the person's circumstances. Compassion evokes empathy, often coupled with a desire to help in some way. We can offer to assist, but we shouldn't automatically assume our help is needed, nor to what extent.

## THE MOST LASTING IMPACT
I feel gratitude each day to Bobby for his Visit. I play the "What if?" game—and I invite you to do the same. Ask yourself:

*What if I chose this experience?*
*What if I designed events to unfold this way?*
*What might I gain if I stay open to my soul plan?*

❧

*Compassion, not pity*

# Q & A ON LIFE AFTER LOSS

Since Bobby's Visit, I've been asked similar questions repeatedly. I'm sharing them here. My responses come from a mixture of my own spiritual experiences, those shared by others, my time as a crisis counselor and hospice volunteer, and extensive reading of cases involving near-death and out-of-body experiences. These views are not a substitute for a grief therapist, but you knew that already, right? I hope it brings some small measure of comfort.

## GUILT

**I wasn't there to say goodbye. My partner died alone.**

I respectfully suggest it's not possible for a person to die alone. Bobby spoke of the love that filled the room when he departed this life and the souls that were there to escort him. Nothing about his experience unfolded in solitude. He had joyous companions for his trip home; so did your partner.

When we pass, we are surrounded by a loving army of angels, guides, and relatives from our most recent life. I believe this happens regardless of any faith we might follow on earth, or whether we follow no faith. It's the first tier of joy that awaits. In the case of deathbed visitations, those nearest and dearest start appearing in the lead-up to a person's passing, to help usher in a smooth transition.

## REGRET

**Is my friend angry with me? We had argued before his sudden death.**

This concern arises often when the last words shared were not especially loving. It's part of life.

I say gently: When we worry in this way, we're attaching human feelings to the heavenly realm. If we've had an argument or some other unresolved issue with a loved one who has passed, it can help to remember that they can no longer feel earth-based emotions such as sadness, anger, or disappointment. They shrug these off as they pass between the physical and spiritual planes. These negative emotions simply do not exist on the Other Side. However, your loved ones can see you and hear you. If it helps, speak to your departed friend or write him a letter.

## REMORSE

**I didn't keep a deathbed promise. My mother made me vow to look after my stepbrother, who is the black sheep of the family. Sometimes I feel guilty that I don't keep in touch. Then I resent that she made me promise in the first place.**

Families are complicated; they can be a source of joy or pain on any given day. No one can force you to make or maintain contact with your stepbrother. I'd only suggest that if you do, initiate it from a point of joy, not a sense of obligation. The vibrations around these intentions are starkly different. You are each on your own journey, and if they intersect, that is wonderful. But your mother is not angry at you, nor disappointed. Talk to her about it. I believe she can also access your stepbrother's soul plan for better understanding. (By the way, we will also be able to access the chart of someone who caused us pain, to review a soul contract.)

## WISTFULNESS

**I lost my father just weeks before my wedding. I always thought he'd walk me down the aisle.**

I know you must be hurting. A dear friend of mine, Pete, also lost his father shortly before his wedding, and his take on things might be helpful to you. The elder man's frail body had been riddled with aches and pains, and he'd also struggled with Alzheimer's. He couldn't have traveled to the ceremony, nor would he have understood it. As Pete said, his dad was now young, healthy, and enjoying a front-row seat to the celebration. Your father will be beaming with pride and love from the Other Side.

## LIFE SUPPORT

**My brother and I had a pact that we wouldn't allow each other to languish on life support. Then I left town to go on one of those super-strict silent retreats where you're sealed off. He had an accident, and by the time I reconnected, he had been on a machine for days. Will he ever forgive me?**

I believe your brother is enjoying an existence in the afterlife free of any worry, anger, or other negativity. I believe souls have the option to use a coma state to move between the Other Side and earth, as they decide whether to stay or go. I have read of many such cases in studies of near-death experiences. Your brother may have chosen to leave the physical plane while his body still had a heartbeat. I believe he had a panoramic view (literally and spiritually) once there and could plainly understand the constraints you faced in being notified and in returning home. I am certain from his point of view, there is nothing to forgive. He would not want you to blame yourself for anything. Moving forward, take him along on your adventures to distant parts.

## HESITATION

**I like to talk to my little sister, who passed away six months ago. I just imagine she is there. We were always texting or talking. Am I keeping her earthbound?**

Don't worry that asking for signs or talking to your sister might keep her tethered here—it simply can't happen. Nor do we as humans have the power to control what a soul does. They can move easily between Heaven and earth, as they are no longer bound by space or time as we are. They are not ghosts. Ghosts are spirits who choose emphatically to be earthbound (and they can go to the light at any moment—it is always waiting to embrace them).

## ANGER

**My wife took her life after years of depression and several attempts. I feel angry that she left me alone to raise our children. Then I feel guilty for thinking like that. Is she drifting in a void?**

You're describing natural and normal reactions to loss. You deserve support (practical and emotional) to help navigate your loss and your anger as you and your children settle into this new chapter in your lives. I strongly believe that people who take their own lives are not doomed to restless drifting. They are greeted in the afterlife with abundant compassion and understanding. In turn, they gain more understanding of the impact their actions had on their loved ones. Talk to her, with any emotion you feel at the time. She will meet your understandable anger with love, peace, and understanding.

## PLAYING FAVORITES

**Ten months ago, I lost my mom and my brother in an accident. Obviously, I miss them both, but the truth is, I miss my mom a lot more. I talk to her and dream about her. Anytime I'm alone in the car, that's our time. Does my brother know? Does it make him sad or mad?**

I believe that when we arrive on the Other Side, we joyfully shed our earthly bodies—and along with that, our naturally limited human perspective. Your brother is no longer able to feel sadness, nor does he have any need for it. The very "air" he breathes is infused with love and kindness. He not only breathes love, he *is* love. The way we might perceive relationships on earth is starkly different to how they exist on the Other Side.

## LAUGHTER

**Recently, my best friend died in an accident. I am heartbroken. But then from time to time, I'll laugh out loud at something like a viral video or a movie. Then I feel guilty. How soon is too soon to laugh again?**

Your friend doesn't gauge your love for her by your misery. She gains nothing from seeing you mired in grief. Enjoy a good laugh. She wants you to feel happiness, just as she feels it.

# GLOSSARY

**Afterlife:** a destination after physical death, be it a place or a state of mind. Also known as Heaven, Paradise, the Other Side.

**Agnostic:** a person who does not know if a god or higher deity exists, or who believes it is not possible to know of any such existence.

**Akashic Records (also, The Book of Life):** a record of every thought, word, or deed associated with each human life; the destination where soul plans are recorded; a collective consciousness.

**All Saints' Day:** a Christian festival celebrating saints in Heaven.

**Almshouse:** an accommodation for the poor, often run by charities or faith-based groups.

**Angel guides:** angelic beings who guide souls on their journeys.

**Atheist:** a person who does not believe in a god or higher deity.

**Bashert:** a soul mate. The Jewish/Yiddish term carries spiritual and religious significance beyond a solely romantic interest.

**Crossing over:** physical death; the belief and process of a spirit passing from earth to the Other Side.

**Divine balance (also, divine order):** the sense of harmony that reigns on the Other Side, as opposed to earth, where duality (such as good and evil) exists.

**Empathy:** the ability or insight to feel someone else's reaction or emotion; to imagine walking in another's shoes.

**Exit points:** off-ramps, or potential points of death, pre-planned into a soul chart as a way to end a life at a particular age or stage. These may or may not be acted upon by the soul.

**Free will:** freedom of thought and action; one's ability to act as a free agent versus being ordained to follow a predetermined path.

**Guru:** a person revered as a master in their given field of expertise; often refers to a spiritual teacher.

**Home:** an alternative term for the Other Side or afterlife.

**Incarnation:** one human lifetime (believed by some to be one in a series of lifetimes).

**Intent:** the willful desire that directs our thoughts, words, or actions.

**Intuition:** an inner knowing or inner "voice"; a gut feeling.

**Karma:** the balancing of life experience through positive and negative events; cause and effect of thoughts, words, or behavior. Often mistakenly associated with punishment.

**Life theme:** a main area of character development that a soul chooses to focus on in an upcoming life. Examples include patience, anger management, or self-worth.

**Life review:** an event after physical death in which a soul sees and relives their most recent earthly life. This is commonly experienced as a movie, with a panoramic view. Some people report seeing events replay from the perspective of others whom they helped or hindered.

**Near-death experience (NDE):** an experience at the brink of death, in which a person "crosses over" and glimpses the

Other Side. Common features include traveling through a tunnel, seeing a light, hearing unusual noise or buzzing, or reunions with deceased loved ones.

**Other Side:** a destination after physical death, be it a place or a state of mind. Also known as Heaven or the afterlife.

**Out-of-body experience (OBE):** the experience of leaving one's body, which often involves viewing one's physical self from above, sometimes with emotional detachment.

**Past life:** a previous earthly incarnation.

**Peyot:** sidelocks of hair worn by Jewish men, often long and curly.

**Pre-birth planning (also, soul planning):** the process whereby a soul designs his or her life before being born.

**Pre-death:** the final hours and days of a person's life before physical death occurs.

**Premonition:** an intuitive feeling or experience that foresees a later occurrence.

**Rebirth:** the act whereby a soul chooses to be born again in the earthly realm.

**Reincarnation:** the process whereby a soul returns to earth for multiple lifetimes, for the purpose of learning and spiritual development.

**Reunion:** the experience of reuniting with the souls of loved ones and pets upon crossing over to the Other Side. This meeting includes loved ones from past lives.

**Samsara:** the cycle of rebirth.

**Second-child syndrome:** a second-born or subsequent child's belief that their worth or accomplishments are valued less than those of the firstborn child.

**Secondary infertility:** an inability to conceive for at least twelve months after having had one or more children.

**Soul chart (also, chart):** the intricate record of a soul's intent for an upcoming life, as set forth in the Akashic Records.

**Soul contract:** an agreement made between souls for the purpose of spiritual growth.

**Soul group:** a collection of souls who travel together, enacting widely varied roles through a series of lifetimes for the purpose of spiritual growth.

**Soul planning (also pre-birth planning):** the process whereby a soul designs his or her life before being born.

**Spirit guides:** wise, benevolent beings who have previously lived on earth and now serve others on their journeys.

**Spiritually transformative experience (STE):** a spiritual experience that has a profound effect on the individual concerned.

**Subset soul groups:** smaller groups of souls within a larger soul group.

**Veil of Forgetfulness (also, the Veil):** the border between physical and nonphysical dimensions. "Forgetfulness" refers to the belief that when a soul passes through this border, it will forget its soul plan and its own divinity, to more fully experience human life.

**Xenoglossia (also, xenoglossy):** the ability to speak foreign languages, including so-called "dead" languages and obscure dialects, to which one has never been exposed.

# SUGGESTED READINGS

## BOOKS

Alexander, Eben. *Proof of Heaven: A Neurosurgeon's Journey into the Afterlife*. New York: Simon & Schuster, 2012.

Anderson, George, and Andrew Barone. *Lessons from the Light: Extraordinary Messages of Comfort and Hope from the Other Side*. New York: Berkley Books, 2000.

Atwater, P. M .H. *Beyond the Light: What Isn't Being Said about Near Death Experience*. Rev. ed. Kill Devil Hills, NC: Transpersonal Publishing, 2009.

———. *Near-Death Experiences: The Rest of the Story; What They Teach Us about Living, Dying, and Our True Purpose*. New York: MJF Books, 2011.

Bowman, Carol. *Children's Past Lives: How Past Life Memories Affect Your Child*. New York: Bantam, 1998.

———. *Return from Heaven: Beloved Relatives Reincarnated within Your Family*. New York: HarperTorch, 2001.

Brinkley, Dannion. *Saved by the Light: The True Story of a Man Who Died Twice and the Profound Revelations He Received*. With Paul Perry. New York: HarperOne, 2008. First published 1994 by Villard.

Browne, Sylvia. *Blessings from the Other Side: Wisdom and Comfort from the Afterlife for This Life*. With Lindsay Harrison. New York: New American Library, 2000.

———. *Life on the Other Side: A Psychic's Tour of the Afterlife*. With Lindsay Harrison. New York: New American Library, 2000.

Chapian, Marie. *Angels in Our Lives: Everything You've Ever Wanted to Know about Angels and How They Affect Your Life.* Shippensburg, PA: Destiny Image Publishers, 2006.

De Angelis, Michelle, and Ezio De Angelis. *Postcards from the Other Side: True Stories of the Afterlife.* Sydney: Allen & Unwin, 2012.

Eadie, Betty J. *Embraced by the Light: What Happens When You Die?* London: Element, 2003. First published 1992 by Gold Leaf Press (Placerville, CA).

Hardo, Trutz. *Children Who Have Lived Before: Reincarnation Today.* London: Rider, 2005. Originally published as *Reinkarnation aktuell* (Güllesheim, Germany: Silberschnur, 2000).

Harris, Trudy. *Glimpses of Heaven: True Stories of Hope and Peace at the End of Life's Journey.* New York: Fall River Press, 2008.

Kübler-Ross, Elisabeth. *On Death and Dying: What the Dying Have to Teach Doctors, Nurses, Clergy and Their Own Families.* New York: Macmillan, 1969. Reprint, New York: Scribner, 2014.

Lupien, Debbra. *Akasha Unleashed: The Missing Manual to You.* Cresco, PA: Self-published, 2017.

Moody, Raymond A. *Glimpses of Eternity: Sharing a Loved One's Passage from This Life to the Next.* With Paul Perry. New York: Guideposts, 2010.

———. *Life After Life.* 25th anniversary edition. San Francisco: Harper, 2001. First published 1975 by Mockingbird Books (Atlanta).

Moorjani, Anita. *Dying to Be Me: My Journey from Cancer, to Near Death, to True Healing.* Carlsbad, CA: Hay House, 2012.

Morse, Melvin. *Parting Visions: Uses and Meanings of Pre-Death, Psychic, and Spiritual Experiences.* With Paul Perry. New York: Villard, 1994.

Myss, Caroline. *Sacred Contracts: Awakening Your Divine Potential.* New York: Three Rivers Press, 2002.

Neal, Mary C. *To Heaven and Back: A Doctor's Extraordinary Account of her Death, Heaven, Angels, and Life Again; A True Story.* Colorado Springs, CO: Waterbrook 2012.

Newton, Michael. *Journey of Souls: Case Studies of Life between Lives.* 5th ed. St. Paul, MN: Llewellyn Publications, 2003. First published 1994.

Richelieu, Peter. *A Soul's Journey.* San Francisco: Thorsons, 1996. First published 1973 by Doubleday (New York).

Shroder, Tom. *Old Souls: Compelling Evidence from Children Who Remember Past Lives.* New York: Fireside, 2001.

Schwartz, Robert. *Your Soul's Gift: The Healing Power of the Life You Planned Before You Were Born.* Chesterland, OH: Whispering Winds Press, 2012.

———. *Your Soul's Plan: Discovering the Real Meaning of the Life You Planned Before You Were Born.* Berkeley, CA: Frog Books, 2009.

Smartt, Lisa. *Words at the Threshold: What We Say as We're Nearing Death.* Novato, CA: New World Library, 2017.

Stemman, Roy. *Reincarnation: Trues Stories of Past Lives.* London: Piatkus, 1997.

Stevenson, Ian. *Children Who Remember Past Lives: A Question of Reincarnation.* Rev. ed. Jefferson, NC: McFarland, 2001.

———. *Twenty Cases Suggestive of Reincarnation.* 2nd edition, rev. and enlarged. Charlottesville, VA: University of Virginia Press, 1980. First published 1966.

Telpner, Heidi. *One Foot in Heaven: Journey of a Hospice Nurse.* Self-published, CreateSpace, 2008.

Van Praagh, James. *Talking to Heaven: A Medium's Message of Life After Death.* New York: Signet, 1997.

Walsch, Neale Donald. *Conversations with God, Book One: An Uncommon Dialogue.* London: Hodder Paperback, 1997.

Webster, Richard. *Spirit Guides and Angel Guardians: Contact Your Invisible Helpers.* St. Paul, MN: Llewellyn Publications, 1998. Reprint, 2003.

Weiss, Brian L. *Many Lives, Many Masters: The True Story of a Prominent Psychiatrist, His Young Patient, and the Past-Life Therapy That Changed Both Their Lives.* New York: Fireside, 1988. Reprint, 2012.

Zukav, Gary. *The Seat of the Soul.* 25th anniversary edition with study guide. New York: Simon & Schuster, 2014. First published 1989.

## ONLINE RESOURCES

The Center for Akashic Studies. See lindahowe.com.

Edgar Cayce's Association for Research and Enlightenment (A.R.E.). See edgarcayce.org.

The Final Words Project. See finalwordsproject.org.

International Association for Near Death Studies. See iands.org.

The Life After Life Institute. See lifeafterlife.com.

Near-Death Experience Research Foundation. See nderf.org.

The University of Heaven with Dr. Raymond Moody. See theuniversityofheaven.com.

Dr. Brian L. Weiss. See brianweiss.com.

# ACKNOWLEDGMENTS

There is a saying in broadcast news: "If you look back on old samples of your work without cringing or laughing, you likely haven't learned much."

The same applies to writing. I wince to read early drafts of this book. I offered my fledgling manuscript to advance readers, and thanks to their feedback, I see now the fuller explanations it needed. They made time to circle passages, jot questions, or point me to related research—amid the demands of toddlers, aging parents, running businesses, carpooling, office deadlines, and other obligations as varied as they are nonnegotiable.

In many ways, this was my most challenging book to date. The support of these friends and colleagues is immeasurable, and my heart is full.

## SUPPORT TEAM

Special thanks to Laura for her spiritual insight and the discussions we share; to Christina for her ongoing support; to Grace for articulating life after loss so beautifully; to Tirza for her thoughtful outlook and key consultation on Judaism; to Tania for her focused questions and for helping me clarify salient points; to Ihaan for his fresh perspective and the passages he inspired me to revisit; to Pingkan for her crucial hospice experience and willingness to wade in; to Leslie for her valued input as a voracious reader; to Howard for raising pertinent issues; to Angela for sending detailed notes, even as she packed for a trip to an elephant sanctuary!; to Jacquie for her feedback and media eye; to Jenny for helping me navigate the timing and approach to this book journey; to Sandy for her ongoing support—and for knowing years ago that spiritual books were in my future!

And, most of all, to Jon. The sound of your key in the door will always be one of my favorite things.

## PRODUCTION TEAM

To editor Theresa Duran for her humor, allergy to error, and a trained eye that could just as well have been deployed in espionage; to designer Lynn Bell of Monroe Street Studios for her delightful interior, which infuses whimsy and substance, and for her creative, inspired cover design; to indexer Amy Apel for her beautifully crisp index and for being so easy to work with; to ebook designer Elizabeth Beeton of b10mediaworx for her intuitive formatting and technical expertise that ensure our digital versions flow.

## SPECIAL THANKS

To Raymond Moody, who brought near-death and out-of-body experiences into the mainstream, for making time to read the manuscript amid all the other demands on his time and energy; to Rob Schwartz, whose painstaking research opened us to the beauty and wonder of pre-birth planning, for his grace and encouragement amid a hectic international schedule; to Lisa Smartt, whose compelling work gifts us with a pivotal road map to our loved ones' final messages, for her support while upholding a punishing calendar and launching the University of Heaven; to Jody Long, whose illuminating work in the field of near-death and out-of-body research fosters both education and community, for her valued input and her encouragement in my spiritual writing journey; to mediums Ezio and Michelle De Angelis, whose work brings so much comfort to others, for carving out time on the road to offer insight and support; to Trudy Harris, whose wealth of hospice experience ushers in smoother transitions, for her immediate warmth and camaraderie.

# ABOUT THE AUTHOR

Alicia Young is an Australian television journalist with more than twenty years' experience in local, national, and international news. Her passion for current events propelled her to Russia (where she presented the news in Moscow), the US, UK, and Europe. She has contributed to newsrooms around the world as an anchor, medical reporter, and international correspondent. She has worked with Walter Cronkite (and was suitably terrified), filed live reports from Rome on the death of Pope John Paul II, covered various presidential elections/inaugurations, and reported on the aftermath of the magnitude 8.8 earthquake that rocked Chile in 2010.

Prior to journalism, Alicia was a social worker and crisis counselor in the areas of child protection and mental health.

Alicia was once told off by Mother Teresa for not having children (she forgot) and has volunteered at a hospice and leprosy hospital in India. Outside work, Alicia handles parasols and power tools with equal ease (not really, but she helpfully holds the flashlight while her better half fixes things around the house).

Learn more at aliciayoung.net.

# SPEAKING ENGAGEMENTS

Alicia is a dynamic and engaging speaker, drawing on her global travel and background in television and radio news to weave a story around a range of topics. She welcomes inquiries for speaking opportunities throughout Australia, the US, and around the world.

# ORDERS AND BULK PURCHASES

*Visit from Heaven* is available as both an ebook and soft-cover. For bulk print orders of any of Alicia's titles, please contact Parasol Press. Bulk purchases are available to community groups, schools, and organizations to present as gifts to their members, students, or conference attendees. Copies can also be purchased wholesale in order to raise both funds and awareness.

### CONTACT
Parasol Press
PO Box 6254, Swanbourne, WA, Australia 6010
Asheville, NC, USA 28805
info@parasolpress.net

# A REQUEST

If you have a moment, I'd very much appreciate a quick Amazon review. You can find a link on my website, aliciayoung.net.

Thank you.

# MY NEXT BOOK—
# AND HOW YOU CAN PLAY A PART

My upcoming book will focus on signs from our angels, spirit guides, and loved ones. In preparation, I'm collecting true, unpublished stories of signs from the Other Side—and I would love to hear from you. Messages of love, reassurance, and inspiration: whatever has touched you. In fact, this is one topic for which I will *always* be collecting stories.

If you one day find this book, dog-eared and yellowed with age, get in touch.

If you spot a copy waterlogged on a park bench, email me.

If you discover a paperback left behind on a plane, drop a line.

In short, there is no expiration date; I will always want to hear from you.

### CONTACT
Alicia Young
info@aliciayoung.net
@AliciaWriter    @AliciaYoungAU

# THE 12 STAMPS PROJECT
## (Because we're more logged on than ever, but less connected)

The 12 Stamps Project taps the power of the handwritten word and boosts literacy. It's vital in this digital age, when it seems we're surgically attached to our screens. Someone in your life needs to hear from you; rediscover the impact of a card or letter on others.

Buy twelve stamps and commit to sending twelve notes this year. Jot a few lines to someone whose advice or practical help made a difference, whether yesterday or in your childhood. Comfort someone who is navigating change, loneliness, or the stress of a job hunt. Share a joke, a quirky observation, or a passionate opinion.

## HOW DO I GET STARTED?

All it takes is the stamps, paper, and a few minutes. Some people start a small group at work, their after-school club, or sorority, while others distribute the stamps among family members.

An easy way to make a child feel important? Send them mail! Write to your niece, nephew, or teen cousin. Tell them that you've noticed how well they share, or the confident reader they've become, or how much they'll love college. We've seen everyone from first graders to professional athletes swell with pride. And a child or teen who receives a letter is more likely to write one; this is a powerful life skill for everything from a thank-you note to a job application.

Do you recall a special note that boosted you? Maybe it celebrated a milestone or a small act that still resonates for you. Share your ideas at @12stamps—we'd love to hear from you!

# THE MOTHER TERESA EFFECT
## WHAT I LEARNED VOLUNTEERING FOR A SAINT

### What's it like to meet a future saint?
### To work for one?

Mother Teresa's mission to the poor resonated through every country, faith, income level, and worldview. Her compassion touched everyone from small children to heads of state—and one garden-variety Catholic.

Journalist Alicia Young volunteered in Calcutta (now Kolkata) over Mother's final Christmas in 1996. She divided her time between Kalighat, the Home for the Dying Destitute, and a rural leprosy hospital. In *The Mother Teresa Effect*, she narrates her transformative journey with humanity, color, and gentle humor.

As the world celebrates the newly canonized Saint Teresa, Alicia vividly:

- Reveals meeting her—an encounter that veered into unexpected territory
- Recounts daily life at the hospice and leprosy ward
- Explains how a one-time go-go dancer coped with living in a convent
- Chronicles daily life in Calcutta, from pavement dwellers to elegant soirees
- Relates anecdotes from others who have felt Saint Teresa's ripple effect
- Shares simple, potent lessons she learned on gratitude and nonjudgment

For more information about this award-winning title,
visit aliciayoung.net.

# TWO EGGS, TWO KIDS
## AN EGG DONOR'S ACCOUNT OF FRIENDSHIP, INFERTILITY & SECRETS

**Alicia Young doesn't have kids. (She forgot.)**
**Yet she has two biological children.**

*Two Eggs, Two Kids* shares how Alicia came to donate her eggs to two couples—both good friends. The way these families began and unfolded are starkly different. One baby's origins were celebrated in the open; the other's, cloaked in secrecy.

Discover a touching and gently humorous look into the world of infertility, experienced by one in eight couples today. Meet:

- Alicia, the egg donor, who explains why she did it—and how
- Angela, one of the egg recipients, who recounts her journey
- Rachael, Angela's daughter, who discusses her "spare mom"

A Guided Tour to Being an Egg Donor:

- What to expect: the physical and emotional assessment
- Questions for donors/recipients and tips for friends
- Anecdotes from donors, recipients, and family members

*An easy read for a potential egg donor, recipient, or their family/friends.*
Lynn Westphal, MD, FACOG, Stanford University Medical Center

*A real, conversational account . . . insightful and thought provoking.*
Lauren Haring, RN, Director of Nursing, Genetics & IVF Institute (givf.com)

*A refreshing perspective on the journey to being an egg donor.*
Gail Sexton Anderson, EdM, Founder, Donor Concierge
(donorconcierge.com)

For more information about this award-winning title,
visit aliciayoung.net.

# THE SAVVY BRIDE'S GUIDE
## SIMPLE WAYS TO A STYLISH
## & GRACEFUL WEDDING

### Be a Savvy Bride!

Who gets a marriage proposal in the middle of a job interview? Alicia Young did. *Really.*

Then she nearly derailed her own wedding when she got flustered with the vows. Gazing into the eyes of her handsome groom, Jon, she declared, "I, Alicia, take you, Father Patrick. . . ."

She had almost married the priest.

While ring shopping, she breezily remarked, "Studies show, the bigger the diamond, the stronger the marriage." Jon didn't buy it (literally or figuratively). But years later, they're still happily married—even without a rock the size of an ice cube.

## TIPS AND TALES FROM AROUND THE WORLD!

*The Savvy Bride's Guide* will help you:
- Trim the guest list, control your budget, and still enjoy a decadent celebration.
- Speak fluent "bride," from *boutonnières* to *bomboniere.*
- Sort the key elements, solve the little details, and surprise your parents with heartfelt touches they will cherish.
- Handle family dynamics with the polish of a seasoned diplomat.

See also *The Savvy Bride's Guide: Your Wedding Checklist*
for a handy countdown to the final three months.

For more information about this award-winning title,
visit aliciayoung.net.

# THE SAVVY BRIDE'S GUIDE
## YOUR WEDDING CHECKLIST*

### The Countdown Is On:
### You're Getting Married!

The dress! The vows! The honeymoon! Now you're counting the sleeps until you glide down the aisle, a vision to behold. Everything is set for your big day, right?

Well, almost.

Building on *The Savvy Bride's Guide: Simple Ways to a Stylish & Graceful Wedding*, this checklist will steer you through these last few months, when cheerful chaos can bubble over into stress.

## TIPS FROM SAVVY BRIDES AROUND THE WORLD!
*The Savvy Bride's Guide* will help you:
- Roll with late changes.
- Track RSVPs.
- Sort last-minute honeymoon tasks.
- Pen stylish, easy thank-you notes.
- Keep your sense of humor and make time for each other.
- Reflect on this new chapter of your life.
- Record journal entries and store keepsakes.

For more information about this award-winning title,
visit aliciayoung.net.

*A simple journal with blank pages in which to jot your notes.

# THE SAVVY GIRL'S GUIDE TO GRACE
## SMALL TOUCHES WITH BIG IMPACT—
## AT HOME, WORK & IN LOVE

### Whatever happened to grace?

Perhaps it was the woman who texted through a funeral. Or the girl on the subway, who loudly recounted a drunken hook-up. Or the colleague who chatted between restroom stalls. Have you wondered: *"Whatever happened to grace?"* Does it really exist only in black-and-white movies? Frozen in time?

*The Savvy Girl's Guide to Grace* is a gentle, inner-beauty make-over for anyone who feels rushed. It's about living gracefully in our fast-paced, high-tech world—with humor and anecdotes from your fellow Savvy Girls.

### TAP YOUR INNER AUDREY HEPBURN!

This is not a book about fish forks, napkins, or how to introduce a duchess and a count. It's about tapping our natural elegance to live a more beautiful life.

From college girls to career veterans, whether with family or friends, this book will help you to:

- Live a more savvy, graceful life—and spark a ripple effect in others.
- Transform your relationships with simple, thoughtful gestures.
- Show the world your best self—at work, on vacation, or with a date.
- See that grace is a powerful tool—far beyond being "nice."

For more information about this award-winning title,
visit aliciayoung.net.

# INDEX

guardian angels. *See* angels and angel guides

guilt, 171

gurus, 28, 178

## H

hesitation, 173–174

Hindu beliefs, 27–28

Home. *See* Other Side

horrific events, 141–143, 147–148

## I

impermanence, 132, 159–160

impulsiveness, 120

incarnation, 178

infant deaths, 136–137

intent, 107–108, 163

interconnection, 59, 63

interpersonal interactions, 167

intuition, 161–162

## J

Jane and Joe (Bobby's parents)

   appearances in The Visit, 56–60, 81–82

   future revelations, 65–67

   Jane's crisis of faith, 70

   miscarriage, reaction to, 70–73

   past lives, 46–49

   reaction to Bobby's Visit, 81–82

   soul planning of, 65

Jewish beliefs, 89

Jon (Alicia Young's husband), 29, 76, 77, 106, 148

judgment, 54, 67, 94–94, 113, 167–168

## K

karma, 98–99, 178

Krishna (Bobby's support crew), 60–61, 164

Kübler-Ross, Elisabeth, 90

## L

language on Other Side, 15, 47, 50, 75, 105, 181

laughter, 175

letting go, 173–174

*Life After Life* (Moody), 90

life review, 93–95, 97–98, 135, 158–159, 168, 178

life support, 173

life themes

   caregiving, 118

   defined, 111–112, 178

   overcoming abuse, 119, 126, 141

   overcoming adversity, 115–116

   overcoming privilege, 116–117

   patience, 114–115

   resilience, 114

   self-esteem, 113

   service to others, 117–118

   setting boundaries, 117

"the light," 87, 91

"lightworkers," 124

listening, active, 118

loneliness, 120, 159

long life, 143

## M

*Many Lives, Many Masters* (Weiss), 88

Marian (Alicia Young's sister), 27, 38, 136–137, 160

marriage, 165–167

meditation, 162

"Meeting at Sinai," 89

mental health issues, 123

PS—If you're like me, you scribble in the margins of your books and highlight passages in fluorescent colors (and if you did it this time, I'm secretly thrilled). If you're a neater reader, please consider donating this copy to a public library, or leaving it on a park bench with a note for someone to enjoy it, or slipping it into one of those charming free libraries around your neighborhood. Buying books can be expensive, and you would be helping someone with your gift (a wonderful idea inspired by Rob Schwartz).

PPS—Please consider a brief Amazon review. I will, of course, owe you:
  a) fine wine
  b) Belgian chocolate
  c) the kidney of your choice
OK . . . I can't actually do that, but I will love you forever. Just think of the karma!

Warmly, Alicia